Republican Party
Reptile

Also by P. J. O'Rourke

Modern Manners

The Bachelor Home Companion

Holidays in Hell

Parliament of Whores

Give War a Chance

All the Trouble in the World

Age and Guile Beat Youth, Innocence, and a Bad Haircut

Republican Party Reptile

Essays and Outrages by

P. J. O'Rourke

Atlantic Monthly Press
New York

Library of Congress Cataloging-in-Publication Data

O'Rourke, P. J.
  Republican Party reptile.

  I. Title.
PN6162.076 1987   814′.54   86-26504
  ISBN 0-87113-622-8 (pbk.)

Published simultaneously in Canada

Printed in the United States of America

Design by Laura Hough

The Atlantic Monthly Press
841 Broadway
New York, NY 10003

To
Warren G. Harding
The original get-down Republican

~~~~~~~~~~~~~~~~~~~~~~~~~~~~~~~~~~~~~

"I am not fit for this office and never should have been here."

Acknowledgments

~~~~~~

"A Brief History of Man," "Myths Made Modern," "A Long, Thoughtful Look Back at the Last Fifteen Minutes," "Just One of Those Days," "How to Drive Fast on Drugs While Getting Your Wing-Wang Squeezed and Not Spill Your Drink," "The King of Sandusky, Ohio," and parts of the introductory essay originally appeared in the *National Lampoon.* "Tune In, Turn On, Go to the Office Late on Monday," "Goons, Guns, and Gold," "In Search of the Cocaine Pirates," and "With Hostage and Hijacker in Sunny Beirut" appeared in *Rolling Stone.* "Hollywood Etiquette," "Dinner-Table Conversation," and "Moving to New Hampshire" appeared in *House and Garden.* "Ferrari Refutes the Decline of the West," "High-Speed Performance Characteristics of Pickup Trucks," and "A Cool and Logical Analysis of the Bicycle Menace" appeared in *Car and Driver.* "An Intellectual Experiment" and

Republican Party Reptile

"Safety Nazis" appeared in *Inquiry*. "Ship of Fools" appeared in *Harper's*. And "Horrible Protestant Hats" appeared on the op-ed page of the *Wall Street Journal*. The author would like to thank these publications for permission to reprint this material. The author would also like to thank editors, past and present, for their assistance and suggestions. In particular, he owes a debt of gratitude to Susan Devins at *National Lampoon*, Carolyn White and Bob Wallace at *Rolling Stone*, Shelley Wanger at *House and Garden*, David E. Davis, Jr., and Don Coulter at *Car and Driver*, and Michael Kinsley and Bob Asahina at *Harper's*.

Contents

ix

Contents

A boy is hitchhiking on a country road. A car stops for him, and the driver asks, "Are you a Republican or a Democrat?"

"Democrat," says the boy, and the car speeds off.

Another car stops, and the driver asks, "Are you a Republican or a Democrat?"

"Democrat," says the boy, and the car speeds off.

This happens two or three times, and the boy decides he's giving the wrong answer. The next car that stops is a convertible driven by a beautiful blonde. "Are you a Republican or a Democrat?" she asks.

"Republican," says the boy, and she lets him in.

But as they're driving along, the wind from the open top begins to push the blonde's skirt higher and higher up her legs. And the boy finds himself becoming aroused. Finally he can't control himself any longer. "Stop!" he hollers. "Let me out! I've only been a Republican for ten minutes and already I feel like screwing somebody!"

—popular joke from the 1930s

Introduction:
Apologia Pro Vita
Republican Party
Reptile Sua

The twenty-one pieces collected in this book were all written from
a conservative Republican point of view. There's nothing unusual
about that except that these pieces are—at least are intended to be
—funny. "Funny Republican" is an oxymoron in the public mind.
Sense of humor and conservatism are not supposed to go together.
There are some well-known exceptions—William F. Buckley, Jr.,
R. Emmett Tyrrell, Jr., and Pat Robertson (though there's always
the possibility that Robertson isn't kidding). But Americans usually
think of their humorists as liberals, like Art Buchwald and Garry
Trudeau, if not radicals, like Lenny Bruce. People who read my
essay "How to Drive Fast on Drugs While Getting Your Wing-
Wang Squeezed and Not Spill Your Drink" ask, "How can *you* be
a Republican?"

    Well, in the first place, I was born one. My grandfather Jake

Republican Party Reptile

O'Rourke was—as you can guess from his name—born Catholic and Democrat. But about the time of WWI his first wife died and he remarried. The second wife proved to be insane, leaving my Uncle Joe, just a year old at the time, out on the porch until his diapers froze, and committing other gaffes. My grandfather went to the bishop to get an annulment. The bishop refused. And Grandpa, according to the family story, joined the Lutheran Church, the Republican Party, and the Freemasons all in one day.

The other side of my family was more rock-ribbed yet. My mother's mother, Grandma Loy, came from downstate Illinois. Her father was county sheriff, Republican committee chairman, and a friend of President McKinley's. Grandma thought the Democrats were, like drought and wheat rust, an inexplicable evil of nature that America had done nothing to warrant. She was given to statements such as, "No one's ever so poor they can't pick up their yard." And she wouldn't even speak the word "Democrat" if there were children in the room. She'd say "bastards" instead.

When I was nineteen I embarked on the obligatory collegiate flirtation with Marxism and announced it loudly to everyone. Once, when I was home at Christmas, my grandmother took me aside. "Pat," she said, "I've been worrying about you. You're not turning into a Democrat, are you?"

"Grandma!" I said. "Democrats and Republicans are both fascist pigs! LBJ is slaughtering helpless Vietcong and causing riots in America's inner cities and oppressing workers and ripping off the masses! I'm not a Democrat! I'm a *Maoist!*"

"Just so long as you're not a Democrat," said my grandmother.

But I couldn't stay a Maoist forever. I got too fat to wear bell-bottoms. And I realized that communism meant giving my golf clubs to a family in Zaire. Also, I couldn't bear the dreadful, glum earnestness of the left.

People who worry themselves sick over sexism in language and think the government sneaks into their houses at night and puts atomic waste in the kitchen dispose-all cannot be expected to have a sense of humor. And they don't. Radicals and liberals and such want all jokes to have a "meaning," to "make a point." But laughter is involuntary and points are not. A conservative may tell you that you shouldn't make fun of something. "You shouldn't make fun of cripples," he may say. And he may be right. But a liberal will tell you, "You *can't* make fun of cripples." And he's wrong—as anybody who's heard the one about Helen Keller falling into a well and breaking three fingers calling for help can tell you.

Neither conservatives nor humorists believe man is good. But left-wingers do. They think man's misbehavior is caused by a deprived environment, educational shortcomings, and improper bonding within the family unit. They believe there *are* people so poor they can't pick up their yard. Down that line of thinking lie all sorts of nastiness. Just ask the Cubans.

So I'm a conservative; what else could I be? However, I'm not completely happy about it. Let's face it, conservatives can be butt-heads, too. There are the reborn Jesus creeps, for instance. We should do to these what the conservative Romans did, with lions. But even regular country club–type Republicans can be stuffy about some things—dope smuggling, for example, and mixing Quaaludes in your scotch, and putting your stereo speakers on the roof of your house and turning the volume all the way up and playing Parliament of Funk at 3:00 A.M.

So, what I'd really like is a new label. And I'm sure there are a lot of people who feel the same way. We are the Republican Party Reptiles. We look like Republicans, and think like conservatives, but we drive a lot faster and keep vibrators and baby oil and a video camera behind the stack of sweaters on the bedroom closet shelf. I think our agenda is clear. We are opposed to: government spending, Kennedy kids, seat-belt laws, being a pussy about nuclear power, busing our children anywhere other than Yale, trailer courts near our vacation homes, Gary Hart, all tiny Third World countries that don't have banking secrecy laws, aerobics, the U.N., taxation without tax loopholes, and jewelry on men. We are in favor of: guns, drugs, fast cars, free love (if our wives don't find out), a sound

Republican Party Reptile

dollar, cleaner environment (poor people should cut it out with the graffiti), a strong military with spiffy uniforms, Nastassia Kinski, Star Wars (and anything else that scares the Russkis), and a firm stand on the Middle East (raze buildings, burn crops, plow the earth with salt, and sell the population into bondage).

There are thousands of people in America who feel this way, especially after three or four drinks. If all of us would unite and work together, we could give this country . . . well, a real bad hangover.

P. J. O'Rourke
Jaffrey, New Hampshire
1986

Things
of the
Intellect

A Brief History of Man

~~~~~~

Man developed in Africa. He has not continued to do so there. Previously, all the dinosaurs had died. Paleolithic, Neolithic, and other oddly named men spread. They used fire, but, being very primitive, they used it for everything—food, clothing, and bodily decoration. Caves were painted, also fixed up and furnished in a simple but attractive style. They were ideal for young couples who were just starting a human race.

There was a fertile crescent and a cradle of civilization and several other things that the Sumerians combined to invent writing, though they did not write novels or short stories. They wrote only clay tablets. The Egyptians built very large items out of whatever came readily to hand. Jewishness cropped up and has never been successfully put down. At the same time (or slightly later, counting Phoenicians) there were the ancient Greeks. These were followed by the less ancient Greeks, who were, in turn, followed by Greeks even less ancient than that. The various periods of Greeks can be told apart by how silly the things at the top of their columns are. The less silly, the more ancient. The Greeks invented amateur theatricals and the incredibly long poem that does not rhyme. It was a relief to all when their Golden Age was over. Greek philosophy, however, has survived the ages and gives us such modern concepts as atoms and platonic love affairs where no one gets laid. The most famous Greek, Alexander the Great, was not really a Greek at all. In modern parlance we would call him Yugoslavian. He conquered what passed for the world at the time but was made to give it back. Meanwhile, in China, there were the Chinese. Rome rose and fell. Barbarian hordes descended from wherever it is that barbarian hordes descend from. They burned the library at Alexandria, destroying most of the great literary works of antiquity and bringing a gleam to the eye of anyone who's ever been forced to study the classics. The barbarians, who had time on their hands, invented feudalism, but it proved too complicated to survive anywhere but in the lexicon of liberal social critics when they discuss South America. Christianity, bubonic plague, and use of the moldboard plowshare spread. France had so many kings named Louis that they had to be numbered. The Dominican Republic was discovered by Columbus. The earth was proved to be out there somewhere and round instead of right here and flat. There was an extensive series of religious debates that killed everyone with an IQ over 50. Prague was defenestrated. Poland was partitioned—the Russians still have the part they got. Napoleon menaced Europe. Then he didn't. Industrialization came to England but has since left. There were some more wars, usually with the Germans but not lately because we're friends again. America had a revolution, a great rebellion, a depression, the New Deal, and then some trouble with its young people during the late sixties. Which brings us up to the present: Sunday, February 1, at 10:45, no 10:46, in the morning. Excuse us, but we've got to go out and get a *Times* and fix breakfast for our dates.

An Intellectual Experiment

~~~~~~

Recently I performed an intellectual experiment. I read one issue of the *New York Review of Books* (Vol. XXXI, No. 7, April 26, 1984), then watched one evening of prime-time network television (Monday, April 23, 1984, 7:30–10:00 P.M.). The comparison would, I hoped, give some clue to an ancient puzzle: Which is worse, smart or stupid?

The experiment seemed fair. The *New York Review of Books* is undeniably intelligent, and television is famously thick-headed. I'm impartial. I'm bright about some things. I don't watch television or read the *New York Review*. About other things, I'm rather dim.

RAW DATA

~~~~~~

I began reading the *New York Review* at 3:00 in the afternoon. The lead article was by Harold Bloom, Sterling Professor of the

Republican Party Reptile

Humanities at Yale. It was a review of *Walt Whitman: The Making of the Poet* by Paul Zweig, though that book was hardly mentioned. Mr. Bloom took some five thousand words to say Walt Whitman is a very, very important poet who masturbated a lot.

The piece had many phrases like ". . . the true difficulties of reading Whitman begin (or ought to begin) with his unnervingly original psychic cartography," and contained such Whitman quotes as:

> *O great star disappear'd—*
> *O the black murk that hides the star!*
> *O cruel hands that hold me powerless—*
> *O helpless soul of me!*

Mr. Bloom said, "Only an elite can read Whitman." This may be why I always thought the poet was a self-obsessed ratchet-jaw with an ear like a tin cookie sheet. "How," asked Bloom, "did someone of Whitman's extraordinarily idiosyncratic nature become so absolutely central to nearly all subsequent American literary high culture?" Beats me.

There were eleven other articles in this issue of the *New York Review* and one poem. Some of the articles deserve brief summaries:

Neal Ascherson reviewed *A Warsaw Diary, 1978–1981* by Kazimierz Brandys and *The First Polka* by Horst Bienek. Mr. Brandys was a communist but got over it. After twenty years in the Polish Communist Party he decided that communism, at least when it has Russians in it, is not a good idea. Nonetheless the Solidarity movement caught him by surprise. Now he lives in New York and writes books about being confused.

The First Polka is a novel about life in Upper Silesia. Upper Silesians were troubled because they couldn't decide if they were Polish or German. Then came World War II.

Gabriele Annan reviewed *Colette* by Joanna Richardson and *The Collected Stories of Colette* edited by Robert Phelps. I gather

P. J. O'Rourke

Colette used language beautifully but didn't have anything to say. Ms. Annan had a great deal to say (one hundred column inches). *The Collected Stories of Colette* includes all the dirty stuff but leaves out *Gigi*.

Milan Kundera contributed an essay titled "The Tragedy of Central Europe." Mr. Kundera, who used to live in Central Europe, thinks the little countries there are swell. At least, they were swell before communism with Russians in it. If somebody doesn't get the Russians out of Central Europe (and/or communism) the culture in these countries is going to disappear. Culture is a hard thing to define, said Mr. Kundera, and it seems to be disappearing everyplace else too.

Gerald Weales reviewed *All Faithful People: Change and Continuity in Middletown's Religion* (a group effort). From 1976 to 1981 a group of social scientists studied Muncie, Indiana. Muncie is the "Middletown" where Robert and Helen Lynd did their pioneering sociology work in 1929. Despite oodles of staff, piles of money, help from computers, and time to spare, contemporary sociologists are not doing as good a job as the Lynds. Mr. Weals said *All Faithful People* should be taken with a grain of salt (and some lime and some tequila, suggests this writer).

Some of the articles do not deserve brief summaries:

The Wandering Jew by Stefan Heym was reviewed by D. J. Enright. It sounded like an interesting novel, but by the time I'd finished reading Mr. Enright's exhaustive praise, I was too bored to even consider buying the thing. Michael Wood reviewed two books about Alfred Hitchcock and proved that some people are unable to experience even the slightest of life's pleasures without being thrown into frenzies of analysis. And Howard Moss's critique of the Martha Graham Dance Company's performances at Lincoln Center was a powerful argument that people who like dancing should shut up and dance.

One article I could not comprehend. Charles Rosen reviewed Julian Rushton's *The Musical Language of Berlioz*. When writing contains such asides as "This is how Schönberg is able to reconstruct the effect of dissonance and consonance rhythmically within a nontonal system," I am out of my depth. However, I gathered Mr. Rosen's thesis was that Berlioz's music either stinks or it doesn't.

One other article I could comprehend too well. It was called "Reagan's Star Wars" and in it nine experts from the Union of Concerned Scientists argued that a space-based missile defense system would be expensive as all get out, would make the Russians hopping mad, and wouldn't save us from getting blown up anyway. The experts presented a great number of facts and figures and many long passages of thoughtfulness to support their arguments. But it seemed to me that by using common sense and inductive reasoning based on the history of defensive weapons the same arguments could have been made in two hundred words.

The poem, by Patricia Storance, was called "Illegitimacy." It did not rhyme. The text implied illegitimacy is an uncomfortable state.

Among all this intelligence there were a couple things of interest. Irvin Ehrenpreis reviewed the forty-eight-volume Yale Edition of *Horace Walpole's Correspondence* edited by W. S. Lewis. Walpole, fourth Earl of Oxford, was a creature of the Enlightenment and a vivid and hilarious letter writer who roundly damned the world about him. Mr. Ehrenpreis called it a "style of ironic recoil" and quoted liberally. Ehrenpreis did not, however, address some important questions. What manner of man makes his living by editing forty-eight volumes of somebody else's bread-and-butter notes? Who, at a cost of $2,700, buys a set of books like this? Where do they put them? Did Mr. Ehrenpreis really read them all? And how did he find the time?

Robert O. Paxton's review of Don Clark's de Gaulle biography was also worthwhile. Mr. Paxton argued that de Gaulle had a perceptive and pragmatic vision of world politics and that his behavior during the sixties was not inspired by anti-Americanism or egocentricity. Instead, said Paxton, de Gaulle was very sensibly putting distance between France and the American penchant for turning every CARE package and UN vote into A Great Crusade.

P. J. O'Rourke

It took about three hours to read the *New York Review of Books*. I lay down for a while with a cold compress on my forehead and then began watching television.

Seven-thirty is the official beginning of "prime time." I had a choice of *Entertainment Tonight* on ABC, *Wheel of Fortune* on CBS, or *Family Feud* on NBC. *Entertainment Tonight* seemed to be the name of the thing I was looking for rather than the thing itself. *Wheel of Fortune* sounded a little *too* stupid. I chose *Family Feud*. It turned out to be a fascinating show. Two perfectly normal American families dressed in go-to-church/second marriage/get-a-bank-loan clothes were pitted against each other. They were asked questions but instead of answering them they had to predict the answers that a hundred other perfectly average Americans gave. "Know thyself," said the ancient Greeks. "Know thy neighbor," say the more practical Americans.

The first question was "Name the most time-saving invention." "Washing machine" was the winning answer, and a good one too. Clean clothes are the hallmark of civilization. But "microwave" came in second. Ugh. Delicious food is the other hallmark of civilization. "Car" and "airplane" ranked only third and fourth —possibly an indication of latent provincialism. "Dishwasher" followed in fifth place and "telephone" in sixth. It's a sign of American folk wisdom, this ambiguous attitude toward the telephone. There aren't many Horace Walpoles in this generation.

I could have pondered all this for hours—minutes, anyway—but another question was already posed. "What should athletes *not* do when in training?" "Smoke cigarettes" came in first, reasonably enough. But down the list in fifth place was "have sex," which doesn't hurt athletes a bit. Was this some recrudescent puritanism seeking a fitness-era excuse for itself? Unfortunately at this point I was interrupted by that dubiously time-saving device the telephone. (I suppose I should get a VCR, but the only thing I like about television is its ephemerality.) I was forced to give *Family Feud* only partial attention but did glean that 35 percent of Americans consider pink the most popular nightgown color. By the time

9

my caller hung up, the contestants were playing a word game ("Things used for transportation in the city: . . . bus . . . feet . . .") interrupted by a farty buzzer sound. This was of no interest. But it was disturbing to see American quiz-show contestants applaud themselves when they won. What happened to humble disclaimers and mumbled thanks to third-grade teachers? By the way, does anyone blush anymore?

At 8:00 I had to choose among CBS's *Scarecrow and Mrs. King*, which I feared might be about Stephen King's mother, ABC's *That's Incredible*, which I was sure wouldn't be, and NBC's *TV's Bloopers and Practical Jokes*. This seemed too horrid to pass up, and it was. The hosts were Dick Clark, *American Bandstand*'s master of ceremonies during this century's worst period of popular music, and Ed McMahon, who has some ill-defined role on *The Tonight Show*. They talked to each other a good deal. I believe some of the time they were making jokes.

The "bloopers" were outtakes from television shows where actors and actresses made mistakes. Some mistakes were amusing. An actress named Deidre Hall had a prolonged struggle with syllable #3 in "infinitesimally." The point seemed to be that the famous make mistakes just like the rest of us. The "practical jokes" were all played on well-known people (at least the show claimed they were well known). I was perplexed. The beauty of a practical joke is vengeance. What reason was there to wreak vengeance on these supposed celebrities? Has fame replaced wealth as a criterion of class division? Is being unknown the modern equivalent of being oppressed? Are fameless people therefore justified in rising up against the better-publicized?

One practical joke, however, was telling. Some actress I'd never heard of was escorted into a "butcher shop" to buy steaks for a barbecue. The butcher brought out a live cow, showed the actress where the steaks would be sliced out, then led the cow into a back room. A shot was heard, followed by the sound of a meat saw. The actress was horrified and the audience convulsed. How far we've come from our agrarian heritage.

P. J. O'Rourke

The rest of the show was simply junk, mostly in the form of old television commercials shown for their alleged amusement value. Another, particularly idiotic segment had the nighttime collegiate-humor-show host David Letterman tour an inventors' convention and sneer at people. A Mexican man had created a device to detect signs of life in a casket. Mr. Letterman and the audience thought this hilarious. It may not be such a good joke in a country with poor medical care and no embalming. A black woman had developed a heated chair cushion to keep people warm in chilly homes. Letterman thought this, too, was risible. I'm glad his home is so well heated. I've used a similar item in duck blinds and found it a godsend. The audience laughed whenever foreigners were on the screen. A number of the inventors were oriental and the audience seemed to find that extremely funny. I hope the audience finds waiting in unemployment lines as amusing.

TV's Bloopers and Practical Jokes lasted an hour—remarkable content mileage. Incidentally, whenever any of the befuddled victims said, "Oh, my God," "God" was bleeped out.

At 9:00 NBC and ABC were showing movies, so I watched something on CBS called *Kate and Allie.* As best I could figure, the situation in this situation comedy is that Kate and Allie are two divorced women who've set up house together with one in the role of housewife and the other as breadwinner. There are a number of children. The atmosphere is faintly homoerotic but with references to dating men. In the episode I saw, the breadwinner (I couldn't determine which was Kate and which was Allie) lost her job and the housewife began making money by baking cakes at home. In the end, as per a long-established rule of situation comedy, everything returned to *status quo ante.* The message seemed to be that housewifery and job-holding have equally valid rewards. And some people hate to clean house, and some people hate to have jobs. People should do what they like best, within reason—a fair-minded thesis and utopian in a friendly, middle-class American way.

The movies were still on at 9:30, so I watched CBS's *Bob Newhart Show.* This also dealt with woman's place in society. The character played by Mr. Newhart has moved to a small town in Vermont. The people there are very backward. At a potluck supper all the men ate in the dining room while the women ate in the kitchen. The wife of Mr. Newhart's character took umbrage at this and convinced the women to rebel and eat their potluck in the dining room. They did so but ended up at a separate table away from the men.

I've lived in northern New England for years and have never seen such behavior. But maybe this is what potluck suppers are like in Los Angeles, where situation-comedy writers live.

To be fair, I suppose I should have watched one more half hour of television. But after careful, objective consideration of the evidence gathered thus far, I decided: Screw it.

ANALYSIS

In the two lists below I have attempted to summarize the information gathered from one issue of the *New York Review of Books* and one evening of network television.

INFORMATION FROM NEW YORK REVIEW

1. Walt Whitman is an important poet.
2. He masturbated a lot.
3. He was a hard guy to figure.
4. Communism is bad when Russians have anything to do with it.
5. Upper Silesians couldn't decide if they were Polish or German, then most of them died.

INFORMATION FROM NETWORK TELEVISION

1. Washing machines save more time than jet planes or telephones.
2. Athletes shouldn't smoke cigarettes.
3. Maybe they shouldn't have sex either.
4. Pink is a popular color for nightgowns.
5. Americans do not blush to congratuate themselves.

6. War is bad.

7. Colette's French was good.

8. Colette was a self-obsessed ratchet-jaw.

9. The Farrar, Straus and Giroux edition of *The Collected Stories of Colette* doesn't have *Gigi* in it.

10. Central Europe's culture is disappearing.

11. Russians are bad.

12. Everybody's culture is disappearing.

13. Sociology isn't what it used to be.

14. Stefan Heym has written a novel of genius but it's complicated.

15. Alfred Hitchcock was a hard guy to figure.

16. The Martha Graham Dance Company isn't what it used to be.

17. The Martha Graham Dance Company's costumes are too la-di-da.

18. Berlioz's music either stinks or it doesn't.

19. A space-based missile defense system will be expensive.

20. It will make the Russians mad.

21. It won't work.

22. Atomic war is very bad.

6. Dick Clark and Ed McMahon are entertaining.

7. Actors are human.

8. It's fun to trick others.

9. Meat comes from dead animals.

10. Old television commercials are silly.

11. We're more sophisticated than we used to be.

12. Foreigners are funny.

13. Orientals are particularly funny.

14. David Letterman is funny too.

15. You can't say "God" on television unless you mean it.

16. Traditional male and female social roles are both rewarding.

17. A little lesbianism is cute as long as you date men.

18. People should do what they like best, within reason.

19. Men and women should be equal.

20. Small-town folks are behind the times.

21. Some things never change.

23. It's upsetting to be illegitimate.
24. Horace Walpole was some letter-writer.
25. Charles de Gaulle was playing with a full deck after all.

Percentage of information from the *New York Review* that was news to me: *28%*

Percentage of information from the *New York Review* that sounded like bunk: *12%*

Percentage of information from network television that made sense: *52.4%*

Percentage of information from network television that made my flesh crawl: *52.4%*

Percentage of information from either source that was worth repeating to friends or acquaintances: *10.9%*
   Specifically:
   Walt Whitman masturbated a lot.
   The Martha Graham Dance Company costumes are too la-di-da.
   Charles de Gaulle was cool.
   Pink is the most popular color for nightgowns.
   "God" gets bleeped if you say it on television.

CONCLUSIONS

Whether smart is worse than stupid or vice versa is an important question. Smart means Neo-Expressionist paintings, which are awful. But stupid means music videos, which are pretty awful too. Ignorance is stupid, but education causes college students. Logic is smart, but Marxism is logical. Smart people don't start many bar fights. But stupid people don't build many hydrogen bombs. Then

14

again, smart people would never drop one. Or would they? It's something we ought to know.

The test of the *New York Review* against network television cannot be said to have proved conclusive. However, several working hypotheses did emerge:

A. Intelligence is, in this case, slightly preferable to stupidity because it is, well, more intelligent.

B. In order to get anything of value from the *New York Review* one must shine the cold, hard light of stupidity upon it.

C. Television, to be worthwhile, must be approached with all the intellectual capacity at one's command.

D. If you try to do both in the same day, you will need a big drink.

Myths Made Modern

*Twelve romances from
the Hellenic Golden Age
turned into a dozen
stories about Greek love*

APOLLO AND DAPHNE

Apollo is the son of Jupiter, who is president of the gods, and Latona, an old girlfriend of Jupiter's whom he never married. Apollo is the god of handguns, Blue Cross coverage, and elaborate home stereo systems. Also, he is the god of getting a dark and even tan.

Apollo's first love was a girl named Daphne, and this came about because of the anger of Cupid, the god of interpersonal relationships. Apollo, as befits a god, possesses perfect marksmanship. In fact, it was his celestial hand which steadied the .44 caliber pistol when the Son of Sam murdered all the pale girls who weren't carrying adequate medical insurance. And it was also Apollo who guided the shots which hit John Lennon because of the awful mixing quality on the Plastic Ono Band album. Apollo was chaffing Cupid about that deity's recent change to automatic weapons, which Cupid insisted was necessary to keep up with the fast-paced shifts in modern emotional involvement. Apollo was saying that Cupid could not hit the long side of a supertanker with an Uzi, so Cupid let him have it with one of his deep-felt emotional-commitment rounds. Then Cupid fired a couple of the bullets which make women want careers. And these struck Daphne, who was a beautiful tennis-court nymph. Apollo was immediately smitten with Daphne, but she wanted to go to law school. Apollo followed Daphne around and pestered her and phoned her in the middle of the night all the time until Daphne became annoyed and called upon Diana, the goddess of women who are searching for self-fulfillment, and asked that august deity to turn her into a female Family Court judge. Apollo wept when he saw the transformation. But he still loved Daphne, and to this day, whenever Apollo spies a case of child abuse where the youngster's injuries aren't covered by a private or corporate medical plan, he has the parents arrested and their cases placed on Daphne's court docket.

IO

Juno is the first lady of Olympus and the goddess of acting like a married woman. She keeps a close eye on her husband, Jupiter. One day while Juno was straightening up around heaven she saw a large smog cloud descend over the usually sunny climes of Southern California. Juno suspected Jupiter of causing this smog to conceal some activity of his. So she called upon Zephyr, an arctic air mass high-pressure zone causing local high winds and cold temperatures, to blow the smog away. Then Jupiter was revealed in a motel room with a Datsun. Juno guessed that the Datsun's form concealed some fair beauty, transformed for concealment's sake. And she was right, for it was Io, daughter of the Imperial Valley irrigation sprinkler system god Inachus. Jupiter had been dallying with her all afternoon in the motel.

Juno quickly joined her husband and praised the beauty of the compact car in his room. Jupiter claimed that he had just created it from a bedspring and a room-sized refrigerator unit on commission for a Japanese car company. Juno asked to have it as a gift. What could Jupiter do? He was loath to give his girlfriend to his wife, but how could he refuse Juno such a trifling request as a new Japanese car, especially one which got such good mileage? So he consented. Juno was still suspicious, however, and took the car to Argus to be closely watched.

Now, Argus was a beast with a hundred eyes and at least that many concealed microphones and wiretaps. He worked for the Central Intelligence Agency, even though he wasn't supposed to because its charter forbids domestic operations. Anyway, Argus never slept or at least didn't sleep very well unless he took two Nembutals, which his doctor had forbidden him for fear that he was developing a barbiturate dependency. So Argus kept Io under round-the-clock surveillance.

Jupiter was very upset by these developments, and so he called for Mercury. Mercury presides over big business, professional wrestling, running political campaigns, and illegal dumping of toxic waste—over all things, in other words, which require cleverness, dexterity, and two sets of account ledgers. Mercury is also the United Parcel Service delivery truck driver of the gods and wears a winged cap and wing-tip shoes. Jupiter instructed Mercury to go to Argus and "lean on him a little." So Mercury pretended to be from the staff of a Senate subcommittee investigation and read to Argus from a book of government rules and regulations about clandestine intelligence operations for hours until every one of Argus's eyes closed and he was asleep. Then Mercury had him blown up by a right-wing Cuban expatriate group.

So Io escaped and drove down the highway to Palm Springs, but Juno sent a gas shortage to afflict her and she had to wait for hours and hours in a gas line in Compton, and her hubcaps were stolen. At last Jupiter interceded and, by promising to pay no further attentions to Io, convinced Juno to relent. Which she did, and furthermore Juno even went so far as to get Io a good part in a new thriller movie from Paramount, where we will be seeing her soon in a car chase all over Asia Minor.

HERO AND LEANDER

Leander was a youth from Santa Monica, and Hero lived many miles away in Laurel Canyon, where she was a priestess of Venus, the goddess of mixed doubles, eye makeup, and random rape slayings. Every weekend Leander used to marathon-run all the way from Santa Monica to Laurel Canyon. But one weekend the weather wasn't very good and Leander decided to lift weights instead. And he never saw Hero or called her again. Some weeks later Hero saw Leander marathon-running with another girl, and she was so despondent that she began marathon-running also and now she feels a lot better about herself.

DIANA AND ACTAEON

Diana is the virgin (with men, anyway) goddess of female self-actualization. She is also the protectoress of wives who have shot their husbands in the back of the head with a .38 after fifteen or twenty years of marriage and then get off with a plea of self-defense by saying their spouse used to whip them with a belt.

One day Actaeon, a noted job hunter, was out looking for work and accidentally saw Diana naked, or, some say, even worse, in a pretty, frilly dress. Diana turned Actaeon into an employer, and he was set upon by OSHA investigators who made him post danger signs in six languages over all his drill presses and give every member of his bookkeeping staff a hard hat and build a new $40,000 rest room for women workers with couches where they could lie down if they were having their periods. Eventually he was hounded into bankruptcy.

PYGMALION

Pygmalion was a fashion photographer who was homosexual and hated women. However, he had one model whom he had discovered while she was waiting tables in Redondo Beach, and he fixed her hair and he did her makeup and showed her how to dress, and when he was done she was so beautiful that he fell in love with her even though he was queer. So Pygmalion prayed to Venus, the style and leisure section goddess, to transform the fashion model into a human woman, and—miracle of miracles—it was done. They both lived happily ever after until the fashion model met a movie actor and ran off to Kauai with him.

ORPHEUS AND EURYDICE

Orpheus was the son of Apollo and the muse Car Stereo. When Orpheus was a boy his father presented him with a Sony Walkman and a collection of Bix Beiderbecke tape cassettes. Nothing could withstand the charm of this music. Not only were Orpheus's friends and relatives entranced by the tunes but even the stock market could be lulled into a day of light trading by the fine melodic improvisations of Beiderbecke's cornet and the prime rate could be induced to drop a point or more.

Orpheus fell in love with the beautiful Eurydice, but unfortunately she stepped on a cancer cell during their honeymoon and was killed by a bad movie plot. Orpheus went to the underworld in search of his bride. There he found his way barred by the great three-headed dog Cerberus, who has one head representing inadequate gun control, another head representing unemployment, and a third head representing judicial leniency and backlogged court calendars. Cerberus relented, however, when Orpheus let him wear the Walkman on his unemployment head and listen to "In a Mist." After that Orpheus talked to a number of underworld figures and many of them turned out to be real Beiderbecke fans too. They agreed to let Eurydice out of the movie contract where she had to die from the special kind of cancer that only actresses get (and which lets them keep their looks even after they're supposed to have been on chemotherapy for six months). The only condition was that Orpheus was never to look at the videotapes of what Eurydice had been doing while she was associating with reputed members of organized-crime families. But Orpheus couldn't resist taking a peek, and it ruined their marriage.

PENELOPE'S SUITORS

Penelope was the wife of the war hero Ulysses, who had been an officer in Vietnam. He was overseas for a long time and Penelope felt like he was *never* coming back. So she had a lot of suitors. But Ulysses did come back, and when he did he killed all of Penelope's men friends. And he would have gone to jail if the jury hadn't decided that he was suffering from post-Vietnam Stress Syndrome and therefore had been temporarily insane.

ECHO AND NARCISSUS

Echo was a sauna, Jacuzzi, and hot-tub nymph who never had anything original to say, and Narcissus suffered from a narcissistic personality disorder and was somewhat neurotic. They dated for a while but it didn't really work out. She's got a job now as a production assistant at Lorimar and he's trying to make it as a male model.

PYRAMUS AND THISBE
〰〰〰〰〰〰〰〰〰〰〰〰〰〰〰〰〰〰

Pyramus was the best-looking boy and Thisbe was the cutest girl in all of Tarzana Junior High School. But even though they lived right next door to each other their parents wouldn't let them date because each family thought the other family wasn't Jewish. So the only way Pyramus and Thisbe could get together was at the tennis club or at parties or in school or at the beach or in the shopping mall or at dances or on the weekends.

One night Pyramus and Thisbe agreed to meet secretly on the boardwalk in Venice. Thisbe got there first, but before Pyramus came to meet her she was chased by a Mexican street gang, and as she ran away she dropped her purse. Pyramus arrived shortly, and when he came to the place where he was supposed to meet Thisbe he saw her purse where it had fallen with all of its contents spilled out on the sidewalk. "Alas," spoke Pyramus, "Thisbe has been chased by a Mexican street gang and doubtless raped and will now have all sorts of hang-ups about sex and will have to go to group therapy sessions and also her birth-control pills are lying here on the ground and have been crushed by roller skaters and she's probably not going to want to fuck anyway until she gets the prescription refilled. I guess I'll turn queer." But Thisbe had escaped from the gang of Mexicans and was returning to the place where she had vowed to meet Pyramus just as Pyramus tried to pick up a member of another Mexican street gang. So they both got raped.

On the very spot the three Fates, Clotho, Lachesis, and Atropos—who stitch the cloth of human destiny into slacks and have the cuffs altered to determine man's lifespan—have caused a mulberry tree to be planted with berries red as blood. But this has nothing to do with our story and was the result of an earlier car wreck.

P. J. O'Rourke

PLUTO AND PROSERPINE

Proserpine was the beautiful daughter of Ceres, goddess of farm price supports and of balancing economic development with ecological concerns. Proserpine used to hang around with Pluto, an underworld big shot. They eloped and were married in Reno and then Pluto carried her off either to hell or to the 1948 Democratic National Convention—it being difficult to tell the difference in the matter of smoke and noise. Ceres was wroth. She searched everywhere for her daughter and in her anger she caused wheat rust and weevils and leaf blight and soil erosion and a really incompetent Department of Agriculture bureaucracy under the Truman administration, thus bringing much distress to mankind. At long last the whereabouts of Proserpine came to light during the Senate's Kefauver Committee hearings on organized crime. Ceres sent her lawyer to make a deal with Pluto, and in return for immunity from federal prosecution Pluto allowed Proserpine to visit her mother during the spring and summer at the Ceres family truck farm near El Centro. And that is how the different seasons of the year came into being. Thus, to this day for half the year we have floods and droughts and depressed prices on the commodities market and the rest of the time we have drug smuggling, extortion, murder, and theft.

CUPID AND PSYCHE

The myth of Cupid and Psyche is a difficult myth to understand. Psyche was a beautiful young girl whom the god of liking people a lot fell in love with by accident when he shot himself in the foot. They got married, but it was an open marriage and Psyche wasn't supposed to see Cupid hardly at all. However, as it turned out, she

23

saw quite a lot of him and caught more than a little grief from his possessive mother, Venus. Everything turned out all right in the long run, though, and Psyche was made an immortal by having her picture on the cover of *People* magazine.

The true meaning of this myth can only be understood by spending years in analysis with a Freudian psychiatrist who needs words like "psyche" to explain vague things he probably shouldn't be fooling around with anyway.

VENUS AND ADONIS

Part of Cupid's problems probably have to do with the fact that his mother, Venus, once fell in love with Adonis, a professional skier, and Cupid witnessed that young man's death in a chairlift accident. Venus was greatly grieved and transformed the fallen slalom racer into an eternal personal vibrator. As a result, Cupid still has ambivalent feelings about the active expression of female sexual needs.

Tune In, Turn On,
Go to the Office
Late on Monday

Every generation finds the drug it needs. The 1950s man, the corporate bevel gear, got silly on his dry martinis. The idiot hippie babbling in his pad had psychedelics to make it all mystic and smart. The wimps of the seventies took cocaine for their climb to the top. And the cold, selfish children of 1985 think Ecstasy will make them loved and loving. It's all pet food. Drugs are a one-man birthday party. You don't get any presents you didn't bring. Personally, I haven't taken a new drug in fifteen years. The mature adult—balanced, reasonable, facing the world and the self with a steady eye—doesn't need drugs. Except for one of those martinis every now and then or three or five of them and a line of blow if he's going out dancing later and some champagne and a joint and a fistful of Tylenol, Bloody Marys, Valium, and . . . what the hell, who's got the Ecstasy?

Republican Party Reptile

Practically everybody, as it turns out. "You have incredible insights," said a magazine editor. "Everybody you're with, you just *bond*," said a jewelry designer. "Oh, gosh, tee-hee-hee-hee-hee," said an Off-Broadway actress. "Your defenses melt," said somebody else. I got mine from a Manhattan businessman. He and I, a young woman of our acquaintance, and a Texan journalist took it together.

Another half-dozen people came by that night, and—here's a friendly point about the drug—I cannot tell you which if any of them was high. With one exception. My friend L. brought an earnest, twerpy date who was flat uncomfortable seeing WASPy layabouts blasted on drugs in early middle age. He was wearing a dago sport coat with wedges of cheddar cheese in the shoulder pads and a pattern like bad TV reception. I definitely didn't bond to him and would have needed the aesthetics of epoxy cement to do so. He kept looking like he was trying to remember the poison-control phone number and left early.

Anyway, Ecstasy came in a largish plain pill. It was supposed to be stuff from the pre-illegal days but still looked, to this retired Aquarian, like it had been hand-made on a home tabbing machine. The dosage was . . . forget it. I recall long, lying discussions about mgs and mics in the days when I thought I had a Ph.D. in street pharmacology. But dope comes in just two dosages: too much and not enough. What we took fell in that general range—better than staying up late to watch David Letterman alone and not so good the police had to raid us.

But first you sit around for half an hour or forty-five minutes. Then there's a sort of resigned sigh in the brain. "Yes," you tell it, "I've been tampering with your synapses again. Try to think of it as anger or lust. These, too, cause chemical changes in the cerebral cortex and alter—"

"Oh, shut up," says Mr. Brain.

Then the Supreme Body Court starts deliberating: "Are we going to love this thing or have cardiac arrest? We need to shit, sleep, throw up, dance. Nope. Just kidding. None of those things,

only a big feeling. Not euphoria exactly, not epiphany, just a great
big good feeling."

"Can it," says Mr. Brain.

"Ahhh," says the Manhattan businessman.

"Whew," says the Texan journalist.

"Hmmm," says the young woman.

I say, "Fuck! This isn't bad at all."

I had to be very serious with the door locks, letting people in.
These were a pretty complicated set of knobs and chains and other
such technical devices but not beyond the abilities of a bright fellow
like myself welcoming all these *good* people into a swell place like
mine.

Which is something of a drug-induced exaggeration. I mean,
not about the people, they're perfectly good. But I have this *pied
à terre* in New York, or *pied à dirt* is more like it. This is a big
chunk of raw loft space looking as only New York raw loft space
can look—like the planet Neptune decorated by wild hogs. Take
LSD in here and all bets are off. You'd wind up in Winter Park,
Florida, begging geriatric old Mom and Dad to take you to a Tough
Love workshop. But on Ecstasy, the dump turned into party spot
central, a big happy room where you could put your cigarettes out
right on the floor and set your drink down anywhere and not leave
glass rings on the Hepplewhite chiffonier. What a bizarre feeling
to be palpably *glad* that you don't have a Hepplewhite chiffonier.
And I don't even know what a chiffonier is.

I don't think much has been written about "Ecstasy taste."
But even the twerp in the sportcoat was looking nice. Surely he was
a fine person at heart, just uneasy because his Armani jacket
couldn't get Channel 7. Our LP selections ran to early Ry Cooder
and *The Best of Joan Baez*—piped-in elevator melodies for the hip.
Music's the food of love. But what's Muzak the food of? Love drugs,
I guess. Typical bachelor, I'd laid out a deplorable buffet of loose
baloney slices, graham crackers, and jalapeño cheese. We didn't
touch this, so we hadn't completely lost our senses. (A German
pharmaceutical company originally patented Ecstasy as an appetite

suppressant, and they had that right.) Still, there was a lot of misplaced admiration for my efforts. Admiration seemed to be running around unfettered generally.

You get these waves of buoyant jollity. Also, sometimes, you get sick. The young woman did. She weighs a hundred pounds and took the same pill as the guys. We're six inches taller and none of us is going to be asked to pose for Calvin Klein underwear ads. About an hour after the drug took effect she broke out in a cold sweat. Her heart raced. She felt nauseated. This lasted ten minutes. The rest of us just perspired, worked our jaws a bit, drank stacks of beer, and pissed every three seconds.

We sat talking like teenagers, that is, volubly and at length about nothing that can be remembered, curled on our chairs, smiling, rocking slightly, feeling wholesome and completely swell. "Are you okay now?" I asked the young woman. "Sure," she said, "I feel great. I'm having a good time. I like being with these people. But"—she turned that eye of inexorable female preserver-of-the-species logic on me—"I always have a good time. I always like being with these people. So I'm not sure I get the point."

And that's it. That's all that happens. You feel real good.

What is this human need to make fun of something else—profound, important, illegal? According to an overinformative article in *New York* magazine (May 20, 1985), Ecstasy is 3,4-methylenedioxymethamphetamine, an opposite isomer (or mirror image) of the active molecule in some hallucinogens. Chemically it's similar to mescaline and, get this, the nasal decongestant Sudafed. I'd say the effect about splits the difference. To me it felt like a very sophisticated, extremely well-buffered speed. You get the glow without the jitters (or the energy to write term papers). Once any discomforts have passed, the only bad parts of the buzz are a mad passion for cigarettes and that grimy feeling on the skin common to many drugs. There's no difficulty "maintaining." If Delta Force banged on your door you'd be able to calmly explain that the PLO terrorists live upstairs in 5B, not at your house.

P. J. O'Rourke

Though you might also thank the commanding officer for being who he is and tell him his uniform is cute.

I suppose you could freak out if you really tried. In the *New York* article, Dr. Ronald Siegal, a pharmacologist at UCLA, says, "We had a psychotherapist who took it, disappeared, and turned up a week later directing traffic." Finally found a meaningful career, I'd say.

On the other hand, there have been claims that Ecstasy provides "instant psychoanalysis." In a *Life* magazine article, "The Trouble with Ecstasy" (August 1985), an unnamed psychologist says, "A five-hour session can be equivalent to five months of regular therapy. It could put people like me out of business." Probably a good idea to put people like him out of business, but I don't see what that has to do with drugs.

What about insights? People keep telling me they had insights, "real insights that really stick with you." But they'll never tell me what those insights were. Are we talking about high-quality insights like the second law of thermodynamics or the Pythagorean theorem? Or are we talking about "I finally realized that, deep down inside, I'm me"? Nobody will say. Myself, I didn't come up with a unified field theory or anything.

To really enjoy drugs you've got to want to get out of where you are. But there are some wheres that are harder to get out of than others. This is the drug-taking problem for adults. Teenage weltschmerz is easy to escape. But what drug will get a grown-up out of, for instance, debt?

If you think of your mind as an animal act (as good a metaphor as any, since bugger-all is known about how psychoactive drugs work in the brain), Ecstasy gets right in the cage and bangs the anxiety bear on the head with a lead pipe. It has the big cats up on their footstools making like stuffed carnival prizes. And it brings on the adorable fox terriers in party hats who walk around on their hind legs, ride on ponies, and jump through hoops for about four hours.

Then it gradually slips away, and so did my party guests.

I slept fretfully, getting up every single hour to go to the bathroom. The next day the drug was still in my system. A shower felt wonderful. I felt okay. I was a little disoriented, like I was in the next room and couldn't quite hear me.

It's not an aphrodisiac, at least not for men. But when you're crowding forty, what is? I called the young woman and asked, for strictly scientific reasons (sort of), "Did you want to make love?"

"I wouldn't have minded," she said.

On the second day all effects were gone, but I was tired and depressed. X-lag is pretty substantial for such a toy flip-out. A long run for a short slide. "Tune in. Turn on. Go to the office late on Monday."

Man, I come from the days when drugs were drugs. We had dope where one toke would turn your hair long and your folks into raving maniacs at the dinner table. Some of that stuff, why, a single hit could transform a Catholic schoolgirl into Gomorrah on all fours, snuff your ego like a light, rotate the tires on the Great Wheel of Being, and make your eyes lay eggs. See God? Shit, you could get Him down in the hot tub and wash His mouth out with herbal soap. And that was if you split the blotter paper four ways. As for insights, try yage and psilocybin mushrooms mixed with mescaline and Anchor Steam beer. Gautama Buddha his own bad self comes over to your house and writes out the Eightfold Path in lipstick on your bathroom mirror. We had drugs that would give you immortal life for up to thirty-six hours. And what about the time the nine-assed peyote demon peeled the top of my head like an orange and vomited the *Encyclopaedia Britannica* into my empty skull? That's what we meant when we said *high* in the old days.

This Ecstasy is a lap-dog drug. "St. Joseph's Baby Acid," said the Texan journalist. There's just enough psychic twinge to make you think you've done something besides a double scotch on the rocks. And all that stuff about openness and mutual trust and deepening of affections is pretty silly. That's why it would be wrong for me to encourage you readers to try it. You're like a family to me. There's a link, a reciprocal union of loyalty and interdependence between writers and readers. I couldn't do anything to injure that basic human connection. I guess I've never had the nerve to say it before, but I love you. All of you. It's a feeling I need to communicate personally. I'm going to get in my car and drive around the country and give each of you a great big hug—just as soon as I call my Manhattan businessman friend and see if he's got any more of this dumb Ecstasy shit.

A Long,
Thoughtful Look
Back at the Last
Fifteen Minutes

This was an important fifteen minutes for America. It was a fifteen minutes of consolidation, of reflection, and of self-realization. I, myself, realized how hungover I was and that I had to go to the bathroom. Some have called it the "Me" fifteen minutes. "Give me fifteen minutes," I called, when it was pointed out I should be at the typewriter making a living. But it's an oversimplification to view this quarter of an hour solely as a period of self-involvement. I cannot speak for the entire nation, but I was involved with the electric razor, which was all gummed up from someone, not me, shaving legs with it. And I was involved for quite a while with the childproof top on the aspirin bottle, even though I have no children of my own. In some ways this epitomizes the sort of caring with which America was imbued during this nine hundred seconds of history. Many childless Americans have allowed that if the government wishes to require these push-squeeze-turn-dangle-yank sort of devices on the top of aspirin bottles for the sake of the well-being of the children of others, then it's all right with them. They don't care. But I care a great deal and will continue to care as long as those things are also hungover-adult-proof and I have to break the top of the bottle on the edge of the sink to get any aspirin out. I care so much, in fact, that I'd like to do the same thing to the other end of the dirt-nibbler who invented them. And throughout all these minutes many Americans, myself included, were deeply involved with others. With chirpy girlfriends, for instance, who'd already been awake for an hour and were spilling coffeecake crumbs in the bed, and by mysterious emissaries from the apartment building's maintenance staff, nattering in Spanish about shutting off the water. Beyond this it was also the fifteen minutes of the American woman. It was time for the American woman to be heard. "I don't have my diaphragm in." I heard that. "Stop it. You'll muss my hair." I heard that twice.

Yet it has not been a fifteen minutes without problems and difficulties. In certain areas it was a quarter hour of stagnation. Blacks have made very little economic progress since 8:45 this morning. Many of them don't have jobs, and the rest are going to be late to work if they don't hurry up. Also, since various authorities contend that we are losing military might and international prestige by the minute, we have doubtless lost fifteen minutes' worth of military might and international prestige. And what of cultural development? What about progress in literature and the arts? What do we have to show for this last fifteen minutes? Nothing, in my opinion, except one blaringly loud recording of the new Police album, which a certain young lady put on the record player about thirty seconds ago and which I told her I was going to break across her coccyx if she didn't shut it off because my head feels like a Palestinian terrorist attack. It's also been a period of unusual weather. Either that or the people in 19E are throwing things off the terrace again. Perhaps it's too soon to have an overview, a proper perspective, on this extraordinary time. Perhaps we should wait until it's 9:30 and we've had another cup of coffee. Except that's when the cleaning lady comes and tells me to get out of here because I'm getting crumpled-up typing paper all over the desk. Maybe I'll go to a movie. Is there anything more depressing than going to the movies alone in the daytime? I wonder why that is. It's even more depressing than drinking in the morning. At least drinking in the morning has a little thrill of misbehavior about it, and I think I'll have a small picker-upper right now. It's something new I invented. I call it a Chicken Shot. It's like a Bull Shot, but you make it with vodka and Campbell's chicken-noodle soup. Just kidding. Me for a Bloody Mary. It's almost 9:00 now and the sun's over the yardarm. Actually the sun is someplace over Queens, kind of over La Guardia Airport, it looks like from here. In fact, right over the short-term parking lot where, it has just occurred to me, I've had the car sitting for two weeks at about $16.50 a day. Shit. Anyway, you get my drift. There's something sweet/sad about the end of an era. Little angelcakes has left for work. Think I'll just freshen this up. You look back and you think of all the things you could have done, the things you should have said and didn't, like "Where the hell's breakfast, huh?" or "Those guinea jeans make your thighs look like the Alaska pipeline." But what's the use of regretting the past? Let's look forward to what the next fifteen minutes will bring. Probably the mail. I hope not. My tab at Elaine's has cracked five K. Oh, God, it's the Spanish maintenance guy again. What do you mean, the water's off until next Wednesday? Fuck. But it's important to get the big picture. Thirty minutes from now all this will seem like half an hour ago.

World
Politics

Safety Nazis

President Reagan has grappled with myriad threats to the American way and tossed no few of them. The pork and dove barrel in Congress has been silenced. Libya has had an emetic. The air controllers have been sent to bed without their or anyone in their family's supper. And something has even been done about that tired observation "The poor are always with us"—what with the end of busing and affirmative action the poor will be, I presume, mostly with each other.

But there is one menace to western civilization, one assault on the free world, one threat to everything we value which the President has yet to confront. I speak of the childproof bottle top. Now a childproof bottle top is a fine thing for a child who has no job or other weighty responsibilities in life and can spend all day mastering the technique of opening bleach and cleaning-fluid containers (a leisure pursuit much resorted to by children—as anyone can attest who has watched a three-year-old tackle the cap on a pint of bug poison with the agility of a pre-Seiko Swiss watchmaker). But an aspirin bottle equipped with such a device is a Gordian knot to an adult who drinks. Consequently our nation is weakened.

Life is filled with pain and sorrow, which facts cannot fail to touch the heart of any perceptive American. Therefore no U.S. citizen with an IQ over 110 is sober after 6:00 in the evening. Yet we have allowed our country's most effective headache cures to be sealed like the tomb of Amenhotep IV. How can our elite confront Soviet hegemony, lower interest rates without fueling inflation, and draft a viable Law of the Sea treaty when their skulls are throbbing to the tune of the sound track for *Zulu Dawn?* Allen Ginsberg said he saw the best minds of his generation destroyed by madness. I have seen the best minds of my generation go at a bottle of Anacin with a ball-peen hammer.

There's an easy solution to this. Place all dangerous household substances out of reach in a crib or playpen and put the children under the sink. But childproof bottle tops are, in fact, only one aspect of a much larger problem. I was depressed the other week and did not know why. My finances were in no more than normal disarray. The girlfriend and I weren't getting along any worse than usual. I was not under indictment for any felony I could think of. Still, I was blue. Days passed before I realized what was the matter: My car was nagging me. I don't like seat belts. They make me feel like a nineteenth-century sea captain. If the car is going to have a wreck, that's its business. I will not be compelled to stay aboard. Yet each time I demur to fastening this contrivance, the car lets out a horrid electronic scold. And this sound is as nothing compared to the shriek when I open a door with the key left in the ignition. And other rude noises and annoying blinkers are rigged to let me know if I do anything else potentially detrimental to my well-being. Some newer-model automobiles have actual recorded voices which speak about one's feckless habits in the tone used by wives during NFL play-offs. I'm told this is the wave of the future. I predict mayhem. All the pent-up hatreds of those households where husbands driven mad by continuous domestic friction murder spouse and offspring and hold police at bay for hours will now be directed at the family car. Once too often the Malibu Classic will inform a drunken gun nut that his trunk lid is ajar, and pow! This is a serious matter. A new family can be had free through various charitable organizations, but a car costs $10,000.

On the subject of automobiles, something worse has happened to them than their newfound disposition to whine and bitch. They have become boring and abstruse—rounded about with lumpy bumpers and Targa bars and looking under the hood like the back of an Atari game. For those readers too young to remember, a car used to be a simple piece of machinery, something like a very fast rider mower but better because you couldn't mow the lawn with it. You started this up, drove off at pretty much any speed you desired, and then exercised a variety of constitutionally guaranteed liberties, usually by having sex and accidents. No more—nowadays if a car cannot survive a drop from the Gateway Arch and emits any vapors more noxious than Evening in Paris, the federal government won't let you own it, and what they will let you own you can't really drive, because fifty-five miles an hour is the speed at which a spirited person parallel-parks, not motors to Chicago.

Medicines which come practically locked in a Brink's truck, electronically admonishing automobiles, speed limits prudent to the point of cowardice—there is a pattern to these annoyances. I purchased a wood-splitting maul not long ago. Pasted on the head was a lurid sticker instructing me to cover my eyes when doing anything with it and attached to the handle was a pair of nasty plastic goggles, painfully uncomfortable to wear and producing that view of the world called "fish-eyed" (though if fish really did have eyes like that we would be able to go after them with ball bats instead of expensive fly rods). A box of shotgun shells now devotes three full flaps to caveats and counsels advising against almost every conceivable kind of shooting activity and stopping just short of warning you not to own a gun at all. And the daily newspaper, once replete with tales of exciting fire and police department actions, political scandals, and international donnybrooks, is now filled with items about untidiness at toxic chemical dumps, hazardous-toaster product recalls, and the cancer-causing properties of everything good on earth.

Something is happening to America, not something dangerous but something all too safe. I see it in my lifelong friends. I am a child of the "baby boom," a generation not known for its sane or cautious approach to things. Yet suddenly my peers are giving up drinking, giving up smoking, cutting down on coffee, sugar, and salt. They will not eat red meat and go now to restaurants whose menus have caused me to stand on a chair yelling, "Flopsy, Mopsy, Cottontail, dinner is served!" This from the generation of LSD, Weather Underground, and Altamont Rock Festival! And all in the name of safety! Our nation has withstood many divisions—North and South, black and white, labor and management—but I do not know if the country can survive division into smoking and non-smoking sections.

As once anything was excusable in the name of patriotism, now anything is excusable in the name of safety. We will kiss some low place on every dishtowel-head in the Levant rather than have a single breeder reactor on our shores. We will make every lube artist in America learn Japanese rather than produce an enjoyable automobile. And we will all be eating Communist bananas rather than risk a Kent State over Nicaragua. (Unless, of course, bananas are found to cause cancer too.) This is treason. America was founded on danger. How many lifeboat drills were held on the *Mayflower?* Where were the smoke detectors in the Lincoln family cabin? Who checked to see whether Indian war paint was made with Red Dye No. 2? It was the thrilling, vast, wonderful danger of America which drew people here from all over the world—spacious skies filled with blizzards and tornadoes, purpled mountain majesties to fall off, and fruited plains full of snarling animals and armed aborigines. America is a dangerous country. Safety has no place here.

In fact, safety has no place anywhere. Everything that's fun in life is dangerous. Horse races, for instance, are very dangerous. But attempt to design a safe horse and the result is a cow (an appalling animal to watch at the trotters). And everything that isn't fun is dangerous too. It is impossible to be alive and safe. It's very safe to be an inanimate object, but the carbon molecules who were our ancestors chose otherwise, and having once set upon a course of devouring things, we must submit to having other things occasionally attempt to devour us. This is painful, but pain is an important part of existence. No amount of hazard warnings on the back of our hand would keep us from thrusting it into a lion's mouth if that didn't hurt. Lions are in admitted short supply, but the same holds true for whirling Cuisinart blades and oil-burning space heaters. Pain is the body's way of showing us we're bone-heads. A child growing up in an excessively safe environment may never learn that he is one—not until he gets married and has a wife to tell him so. Nor can death be avoided. Death is even more important that pain. Death was invented so we could have evolution. The process of Darwinian selection does not work on things that don't die. If it weren't for death we would all still be amoebas and would have to eat by surrounding things with our butts. Also, a lack of death would result in an extraordinary number of old people and the Social Security system is already overextended.

Therefore it is the duty of every patriotic, moral, and humanistic person among us to smoke, drink, drive like hell, shoot guns, own Corvairs, take saccharin, leave unmarked medicine bottles open all over the house, get in fistfights, start barbecue fires with gasoline, put dry-cleaner bags over our heads, and run around barefoot without getting a tetanus shot.

But I don't know how long we will be able to continue like this. The forces of safety are afoot in the land. I, for one, believe it is a conspiracy—a conspiracy of Safety Nazis shouting "Sieg

Health" and seeking to trammel freedom, liberty, and large noisy parties. The Safety Nazis advocate gun control, vigorous exercise, and health foods. The result can only be a disarmed, exhausted, and half-starved population ready to acquiesce to dictatorship of some kind. I do not know what the ultimate aims of the Safety Nazis are, but the prevalence of flameproof infant sleepwear argues that a totalitarian force is looking to someday use my children as fireplace tongs. Other than that, however, it will probably be a very safe dictatorship without the dive-bombers, tanks, and huge artillery pieces which are the only fun things about totalitarianism.

President Reagan has shown some promise of standing up to the Safety Nazis. James Watt was as dangerous a Secretary of the Interior as we've had in a long time. And a few of the safetyist regulatory excesses of the Carter years have been revoked—the requirement that all full-sized sedans carry a blimp under the dashboard, for instance. But as yet there is little indication that the President perceives the true lack of danger our country faces. Maybe this is because he got shot not long ago. That's fine for him. *His* life is plenty dangerous. But what about the rest of us, the common people crying out for hazard and risk? I hope President Reagan keeps us in mind as he trims the federal budget. The MX missile system looks like a perilous thing, but if that proves too expensive, give us a small increase in Amtrak funding and perhaps we could all die in a horrible train wreck.

Ship of Fools

~~~~~~

I never did get it, what this trip was all about. I stood at the rail of the cruise ship *Alexander Pushkin* staring out at the vast rolling shore of the Volga. Here or there was a patch of grain, not high enough even in late July to conceal the line of furrows plowed straight downhill in the most erosion-producing way possible. And here or there was a skinny cow in an untidy hectare of pasture. But most of the land looked empty, unsown, ungrazed, uncultivated. And all around me were minds just as fallow.

I was on something called the Volga Peace Cruise, a sixteen-day trip to the USSR featuring a nine-day boat ride from Rostov north up the Don, through the Don-Volga canal, and on up the Volga River to Kazan. The 160 passengers were all Americans. Most were antinuke activists and peace-group organizers with sixties leftover looks. Others were products of the Old Left. The peaceniks talked about peace, mostly in terms of atomic holocaust. The leftists talked about peace, mostly in terms of Soviet-American relations. The entire program of the "peace cruise" consisted in the bunch of us talking about peace. And the Soviet government had provided five Russian "peace experts" to talk about peace too.

I asked some of my fellow passengers what the point was.

"Atomic holocaust is the most important issue facing mankind," said the peaceniks.

"Atomic holocaust and Soviet-American relations," said the leftists.

What about dissident Russian peace activists? Was anyone interested in talking to them?

"There is no need for dissident peace organizations in the Soviet Union," said the leftists. "The Soviet Union already has the largest peace organizations in the world. In America dissident peace organizations are important because American foreign policy is prowar. But the Soviet Union is propeace because twenty million Soviets died in World War II."

"Well, if we *see* any . . ." said the peaceniks.

Did anyone expect the Soviet "experts" to say anything everyone hadn't heard Soviet experts say already?

"Soviet-American relations are very important," said the leftists.

Were we going to convince those experts that their government ought to pull its troops out of Afghanistan?

"Huh?" said everyone.

Or maybe the leftists would convince the peace activists to take a more political view of things?

"What leftists?" said the leftists.

FRIDAY, JULY 16, 1982

I was attracted to the Volga Peace Cruise by a half-page advertisement in the February 27, 1982, issue of *The Nation* magazine. It read, in part, "Find out for yourself what's going on in the Soviet

Union capital and heartland as you join *The Nation* this summer on an exciting, affordable Soviet excursion."

I have a sneaking love of the old-time left and that compendium of their snits and quarrels, *The Nation*. Mind you, I'm a registered Republican and consider socialism a violation of the American principle that you shouldn't stick your nose in other people's business except to make a buck. Still, Wobblies, Spanish Civil War veterans, the Hollywood Ten touch the heart somehow.

But, to tell the truth, I'd never met any Old Leftists. I expected them to be admirable and nasty, like Lillian Hellman, or brilliant, mysterious, denying everything, like Alger Hiss, or—best of all— hard-bitten and cynical but still willing to battle oppression, like Rick in *Casablanca*. I did not expect them to be the pack of thirty fussing geriatrics I met at Kennedy Airport, misplacing their hand luggage, losing their way to the ladies' room, barking at the airline personnel, and asking two hundred times which gate we'd have to be at in three and a half hours.

They were leftists all right. In between palsies of fretting, they'd tell you how wonderful the Soviet Union was: Pensions were huge, housing was cheap, and they practically paid you to get medical care. Believe me, you haven't been bored until you've been buttonholed by a seventy-year-old woman who holds forth all afternoon on the perfidy of American foreign policy *and* shows you pictures of her grandchildren. These were people who believed everything about the Soviet Union was perfect, but they were bringing their own toilet paper.

SATURDAY, JULY 17
The ad had promised excitement, and surely entering the Soviet Union would be exciting. The Russians are famous for making border crossing an exciting event. But we just stood in line for four hours. "You can understand the delay," said a lady who had complained all night about everything on the flight to Moscow. "So many reactionary forces are trying to destroy the Soviet Union."

Republican Party Reptile

〜〜〜〜〜〜〜〜〜〜〜〜〜〜〜〜〜〜〜〜〜〜〜〜〜〜〜〜〜

If reactionary forces are vulnerable to understaffing and inept baggage handling, they don't stand a chance at the Moscow airport.

There was only one faint thrill when we handed in our passports to the officer in the little glass passport-control booth. He was maybe seventeen with a tunic too large around the neck and a hat too big by half. He made an awful face and shouted, "Num? Fuss num? Plas oaf burf? Dat oaf burf?"

One of my tour group members had been born in Kiev. She said her "plas oaf burf" was Russia.

"Dat oaf burf?"

"1915," she said.

"When leaf?" hollered the passport officer.

"1920."

"Reason leaf?" he yelled.

I swear she sounded embarrassed. "I don't know. My parents did it."

Then we got on a smoky, gear-stripped bus and rode past blocks of huge, clumsy apartment buildings and blocks of huge, clumsy apartment buildings and blocks of huge, clumsy apartment buildings; through the smoggy Moscow twilight, through half-deserted streets. No neon lights, no billboards, no commotion, not much traffic, everything dusty-looking and slightly askew, and everything the same for an hour and a half.

"Some people," said a leftist lady with orange hair and earrings the size of soup tureens, "say the Soviet Union's depressing. I don't know *how* they can say that."

We pulled up in front of an immense glass-curtain-walled modern hotel, a perfect Grand Hyatt knockoff, and I headed for the bar. It was pretty much like any bar in a Grand Hyatt. There was a big drunk man there, red-faced and bloated. He seemed to speak English. At least he was yelling at the bartender in it. "A glass of schnapps," he said. He got vodka.

"How long you been here?" I said.

"Hahahahahahaha," he said, "I'm from Frankfurt!"

P. J. O'Rourke
~~~~~~

"Scotch," I said to the bartender. "Where've you been?" I
asked the drunk. The bartender gave me vodka.

"Fucking Afghanistan!" said the drunk. Afghanistan? Here
was some excitement.

"Afghanistan?" I said, but he fell off his stool.

SUNDAY, JULY 18
My tour group of leftists met with another three or four groups in
the Moscow hotel. The others were mostly peaceniks. I don't know
how my group got involved in the peace cruise or how I got put
in with them. They certainly weren't from *The Nation*. *"The Nation*
prints too much anti-Soviet propaganda," said a potbellied man
smoking a pipe with a stupid bend in the stem.

In fact, there was no one from *The Nation* on the cruise except
one assistant editor in the book-review department. The excursion
ad had run, I found out later, in large part because *The Nation*
received a commission for each passenger it signed up. The ad had
listed a number of other sponsors: Fellowship of Reconciliation,
National Council of American-Soviet Friendship, Promoting En-
during Peace, Women's International League for Peace and Freedom, and World Fellowship League. A few passengers in the other
tour groups were from those organizations, but most seemed to be
representing tiny peace organizations of their own. And if you
didn't stick socks in their mouths right away, they'd tell you all
about it.

First, however, a visit to Lenin's tomb. It's real dark and
chilly in there, and you march around three sides of the glass case,
and it's like a visit to the nocturnal-predators section at the Reptile
House with your grade-school class—no talking!

"He has the face of a poet," said our beautiful Intourist guide,
Marya. He certainly does, a nasty, crazed, bigoted face just like
Ezra Pound's.

None of the leftists so much as sniffled. This offended me. I
can get quite misty at the Lincoln Monument. And I had to explain

Republican Party Reptile

~~~~~~

who John Reed was when we walked along the Kremlin wall. "Oh, that's right," said the orange-haired lady, "Warren Beatty in *Reds.*" Today she wore earrings that looked like table lamps. "Isn't it wonderful?" she said, presenting Red Square as if she'd just knitted it. "No crowds!" The square was cordoned off by soldiers.

Back to the hotel for another big drink.

We spent the rest of the day on a Soviet version of a Gray Line tour, visiting at least thirty places of no interest. For the uninitiated, all Russian buildings look either like Grand Army of the Republic memorials or like low-income federal housing projects without graffiti. There are a few exceptions left over from the czars, but they need to have their lawns mowed. Every fifteen feet there's a monument—monuments to this, monuments to that, monuments to the Standing Committee of the Second National Congress of Gypsum and Chalk Workers, monuments to the Mothers of the Mothers of War Martyrs, monuments to the Inventor of Flexible Belt Drive. "In the foreground is a monument to the monument in the background," Marya narrated.

During a brief monument lacuna, Marya said, "Do any of you have questions that you would like to ask about the Soviet Union?"

"Where can I get a—" But the leftists beat me to it.

"What is the cost of housing in the Soviet Union as a percentage of worker wages?" asked one.

"What is the retirement age in the Soviet Union?" asked another.

"What pension do retired Soviet workers receive as a percentage of their highest annual work-life salary?"

"Is higher education free in the Soviet Union?"

"What about unemployment?"

Marya answered, pointed out a few more monuments, and asked, "Do any of you have other questions you would like to ask about the Soviet Union?"

Exactly the same person who'd asked the first question asked exactly the same question again. I thought I was hearing things.

"What is the cost of housing in the Soviet Union as a percentage of worker wages?"

And that flipped the switch.

"What is the retirement age in the Soviet Union?"

"What pension do retired Soviet workers receive as a percentage of their highest annual work-life salary?"

"Is higher education free in the Soviet Union?"

Marya answered the questions again. The third time it happened she began to lose her composure. I could hear her filling up empty places in the sightseeing landscape. "Look, there's a building! And there's another! And over there are several buildings together! And here [sigh of relief] are *many monuments.*"

All the time we were in Russia, at every opportunity, the questions began again, identical questions with identical wording. I'm proud to say I don't remember a single one of the answers. Except the one about unemployment: "There is no unemployment in the Soviet Union. The Soviet constitution guarantees everyone a job." A pretty scary idea, I'd say.

Later in the trip, when I'd fled the bus tours and was wandering on my own, the lumpier kind of Russian would come up and ask me questions—not the "You are foreign?" sort of questions but rapid, involved questions in Russian. Perhaps because my hair was combed and I wore a necktie (two Soviet rarities) they thought I had special access to the comb-and-necktie store and must therefore be a privileged party official who knew what was what. I've wondered since if they were asking me, "What is the cost of housing in the Soviet Union as a percentage of worker wages?"

MONDAY, JULY 19

One of the bus questioners stood next to me as we waited to board our flight to Rostov. She looked out at the various Aeroflot planes standing on the tarmac and managed a statement that was at once naive, gratuitous, patronizing, and filled with progressive ardor. "Airplanes!" she said. "The Soviet Union has thousands and thousands of airplanes!"

Republican Party Reptile

~~~~~~

I never did find out what this lady looked like. She was only about four foot eleven, and all I ever saw was a skull top of hennaed hair with a blur of fast-moving jaw beneath it. She had that wonderful ability some older people have of letting her mind run right out her mouth.

"Well," she'd say, "here I am with my seat belt buckled up just sitting right here in the airplane seat and folding my hands in my lap and I'll move my feet over a little so they're on top of my flight bag and pull my coat up over my shoulders, whoops, I'm sitting right on it but I'll just wiggle around a little like this and pull it over my shoulders . . ." For *hours*, all the way to Rostov.

The peaceniks, especially the older peaceniks, were more visually interesting than the leftists. Somebody ought to tell a sixty-year-old man what he looks like in plastic sandals, running shorts, and a mint-green T-shirt with Kenneth Patchen plagiarisms silk-screened on the front.

The peaceniks were sillier-acting than the leftists too. There was a pair of Quaker ministers with us, man and wife. But they were not Quakers as one usually pictures them. They had "gone Hollywood." Imagine a Quaker who came up to you in the L.A. airport and tried to get a donation for a William Penn button. Not that they did that, but it always looked to me as though they were about to. Anyway, this couple bore different last names. When we got aboard the ship in Rostov, a passenger went to return a book to the husband.

"I'm sorry," said the wife at their cabin door. "He's not here."

"But can't I give the book to you?" asked the passenger. "It belongs to your husband."

"We're *not* the same persons," said the wife.

My cabin mate was no leftist. "I'm not pro-Soviet," he said as he watched me unpack a necktie with little duck hunters all over it. "I'm a retired peace activist. I mean I'm not retired from peace activism—you know what I mean." He had spilled a bottle of Camphophenic in his luggage and had gastrointestinal trouble from the food and wouldn't use the air conditioning because it might give him a cold, so all the way to Kazan our cabin smelled like the bathroom at a Vick's factory. Three bus tours after we met he told me, "This country is just like a big club. Did you know there's no unemployment? The Soviet constitution guarantees everyone a job!"

TUESDAY, JULY 20

Fortunately there were other people to talk to. Actually, you couldn't talk to most of them because they were Russians and didn't speak English—what you might call a silent majority. On the plane to Rostov I'd sat next to a fellow named Ivor. He spoke only a bit of English but was a good mime. He got it across that he was an engineer. I got it across that I was an American. He seemed very pleased at that. I should come and stay with his family. I explained about the cruise boat, showing him a picture of it on the brochure. I did a charade to the effect that I'd better stick close to the boat. He gave me an engineering trade magazine (in Russian, no illustrations), and I gave him some picture postcards of New York. We parted in a profusion of handshakes at the Rostov airport.

The boat stayed at the dock in Rostov until midnight Tuesday. They have plenty of monuments in Rostov, too, and tour buses were lined up on the quay. I could hear someone asking inside one of them, "What is the cost of housing in the Soviet Union as a percentage of worker wages?"

I was just being herded into that bus when someone grabbed my arm. It was Ivor. "Come on," he gestured. I escaped down the embankment. We got on a boat packed to the scuppers with Russians and went for a two-hour excursion on the Don. Ivor bought a bottle of champagne and began a labored explanation punctuated with hand-wavings and flurries of picture-drawing in my reporter's notebook.

His father had been on the front lines when the armies of the East and West had met in Germany in 1945. Apparently the Americans had liberated every bottle of alcoholic beverage between

Republican Party Reptile

Omaha Beach and the Oder-Neisse Line and really made the welkin ring for their Red comrades in arms. "Anglish—*poo*," said Ivor, "Francis—*poo*," but the Americans, they were fine fellows, plenty of schnapps, plenty of cognac, plenty of vino for all. And they could *drink*, those American fine fellows. So Ivor's "vada" had made him promise (point to self, hand on heart) if (finger in air) Ivor ever met American (handshake, point to me) he must buy him much to drink. *Da?* (Toast, handshake, toast again, another handshake.)

Standing behind Ivor was a giant man well into his sixties, a sort of combination Khrushchev and old Arnold Schwarzenegger. He was staring hard at me, cocking an ear to my foreign language. He wore an undershirt and a suit coat with a line of medals out across the breast pocket. *"Deutsch?"* he asked me sternly.

"Nyet deutsch," I said, "American."

He beamed, I mean just *beamed.* "Ally!" he said. It was his only English word. He pulled out a wallet with what I guess were commendations and an honorable discharge. *"Amerikanskii* ally!" he said and slapped my shoulder. Eight-ounce glasses of brandy must be bought for Ivor and me.

I toasted him with *my* only *Russian* word—*"Tovarishch!"* He brought forth a tiny grandson and had him shake hands with me.

"Now the little one can say he met an American," Ivor more or less explained. I toasted the big guy again. He pledged a long toast in return, and, as I understood Ivor's translation, we'd drunk to the hope that America and Russia would be allies again in a war against China.

I bought more cognac. Ivor bought beer. The big fellow bought even more cognac.

When the boat docked Ivor and I went to a beer hall, a basement where they lined up half-liter mugs and squirted them full with a rubber hose from four feet away. Everyone grabbed half a dozen mugs at a time and drank one after the other while standing at long wooden tables. There was no communication problem now. We discussed women ("Ah, beautiful. Oh, much trouble"), international politics ("Iraq—*poo.* Iran—*poo* "), the relative merits of socialism versus a free-market system ("Socialism—enough responsible, *nyet* fun. Captialism—*nyet* enough responsible, plenty fun"), and, I think, literature (*"And Quiet Flows the Don—poo,* too long"). Then we went to another bar on top of a Russian tourist hotel and had even more to drink. I didn't want to let my side down. And there were Ivor's father's feelings to be considered.

Ivor and I embraced, and I staggered back to my stinking cabin to pass out. The woman with her brains between her teeth was standing at the top of the gangplank. "I hope you're not one of those people who's going to see the Soviet Union through the bottom of a vodka glass," she said.

THE ENEMY AMONG US

Of course, we had plenty of Russians aboard the boat too. There were five of the advertised experts. I'll change their names in case some reconstructed quote or poetic exaggeration of mine is misconstrued to mean that one of these Soviets might be "turned" by the CIA. No one deserves to be pestered by surreptitious Yalies who couldn't get into law school.

Two of the experts were really journalists. Natalia was a pleasant blond woman of about forty. She didn't have much to say. Nikolai was a sturdy guy in his mid-thirties, completely western in dress and manner. He had lived as a foreign correspondent in Switzerland and Austria for seven years, wore a bush jacket like any other foreign correspondent, and was as bluff and hard-drinking as any newspaper man. I gathered this wasn't much of an assignment. Nikolai took no notes at the peace confabs, and Natalia took only a few.

A third expert, Orlonsky, was a sinister-looking type with a half-Russian, half-Tartar face and slitlike eyes. He turned out to be a bored economist from the Soviet Institute of U.S. and Canadian Studies who was along to brush up on his English in preparation for some academic conference he was going to visit in San Francisco. The Institute of U.S. and Canadian Studies is supposed to have subscribed to the *Village Voice* for six years in an attempt to find out about life in America's rural areas. But Orlonsky seemed to be a look-alive fellow. He wanted to talk about America's marvelous demand-side goods-distribution system and did our Reagan administration economic institutes have screws loose or what? Also, where did our automobile industry go? But the Americans wanted to talk about peace and Soviet-American relations.

Two more official-expert types were Dr. Bullshovich from the USSR Academy of Sciences Institute of World Economy and International Relations and Professor Guvov from the department of philosophy and sociology at Moscow U. Dr. Bullshovich was a lean, dry character with a Jesuitical wit that was lost on his audience. Between formal peace activities he hid somewhere. Guvov was a doctrinaire buffoon who looked like a Hereford cow and was a big favorite with the leftists. "He is not a professor," one of the crew members told me later. "He is, you would call it, instructor. He should be teaching military schools."

Besides the experts there were thirty or more officers, sailors, waitresses, stewards, and cruise personnel. Some of the higher-ranking crew members spoke English but usually didn't let on. They preferred to stare blankly when the Americans began to complain. And the Americans did complain, the leftists worst of all. Between praise of the Soviet Union it was "It's too noisy, too rough, too breezy. The chair cushions are too hard. And what's that smell? This food is awful. Too greasy. Can't I order something else? I *did* order something else. Didn't someone say I could order something else? I'm sure I can order something else if I want to, and, young lady, the laundry lost one of my husband's socks. They're expensive socks and one of them is lost."

Translating the complaints, or pretending to, were a half-dozen Intourist guides. They began to have a haunted look before we were two days out of port.

VERY EARLY WEDNESDAY
MORNING, JULY 21

When I came to, after the Ivor expedition, I stumbled into the ship's bar. We'd cast off while I was asleep, and motion of the boat combined with motion of my gullet. I couldn't have looked well. Nikolai was sitting on a stool next to one of the Intourist guides, a dark, serious type named Sonya. I gripped the bar with both hands and tried to decide which of the impossible Russian soft drinks would be easiest to vomit. "You need vodka," said Nikolai, motioning to the barmaid. I drank the awful thing. "Now," said Nikolai, "how did you get that President Reagan?"

"*I* voted for him," I said. "How did *you* get Brezhnev?"

Nikolai began to laugh. "I do not have this great responsibility."

"How are you liking the Soviet Union?" asked Sonya.

"I'm not," I said.

She was worried. "No? What is the matter?"

"Too many Americans."

Sonya kept a look of strict neutrality.

"I have not met many Americans," said Nikolai. "They are all like this, no?" He made a gesture that encompassed the boat, winked, and ordered me another vodka.

"Not exactly," I said.

"Perhaps they are just old, a bit," said Sonya with the air of someone making an obviously fallacious argument. "But," she brightened, "they are for peace."

"Yes," I agreed. "They are progressive. They are highly progressive. They are such great progressives I think I have almost all of them talked into defecting."

"No, no, no, no, no," said Nikolai.

MUCH LATER WEDNESDAY
MORNING, JULY 21

We docked on a scruffy island somewhere up near Volgadonsk. One of the U.S. peace experts, a pacifist from the American Friends

Republican Party Reptile

Service Committee, got up a volleyball game against the crew. "Now let's play and let's play hard," he told the American team. "But don't forget we're playing for *fun.*" The Russians trounced them.

That night the Russians took me out onto the darkened fantail, where they had dozens of bottles of beer, cheese, bread, and a huge salted fish.

Sonya was concerned about my Republicanism. "You are not for peace?" she asked.

"I during Vietnam War struggle for peace very much [talk with the Russians for a while and you fall into it too], rioting for peace, fighting police for peace, tear-gassed for peace," I said. "I am tired of peace. Too dangerous."

Orlonsky began to laugh and then shook his head. "Vietnam —too bad."

"Land war in Asia," I said, "very bad. And some countries do not learn from an example." All of them laughed.

"And in Middle East," said Sonya, mirthfully pointing a finger at me, "some people's allies do not learn also."

"War is very bad," said Nikolai. "Maybe U.S. and Soviet Union go to war over Lebanon—ha, ha!" This seemed to be a hilarious idea. The Russians all but fell out of their chairs.

"With all of Middle East how do you pick only ally without oil?" said Orlonsky.

I said, "With all of Europe how do you pick Poland?"

"You wish to make trade?" said Nikolai.

"Also, in deal, you can have South Africa," I said.

"We will tell Reagan you are a progressive," said Orlonsky.

"P. Cheh. [P.J.] was making faces at the *Pravda* news today. I do not think he is a progressive," said Sonya.

"Oh, he is a progressive," said Nikolai. "You remember, Sonya, he has almost all Americans on ship ready to defect."

Marya made a strangled noise in the back of her throat. Sonya turned very sober. "Progressives," she sighed. "Everything must be made perfect for them."

P. J. O'Rourke

THURSDAY, JULY 22

Our first scheduled conference took place while we sailed through the remarkably scum-filled Tsimlyansky Reservoir. The conference coordinator was a short, broad, overvigorous American woman in her sixties. Let's call her Mrs. Pigeon, so she won't sue, and also because too much truth doesn't go with travel writing. Mrs. Pigeon was an authority on the education of children, and, in fact, had the personality of a teacher—the sort of teacher who inspires any feeling child to sneak back in school at night and spray-paint the halls with descriptions of the human love act.

Mrs. Pigeon introduced the Soviet experts and their two American counterparts, Reverend Bumphead (not his real name) and the volleyball coach, Nick Smarm (not his real name). Nick was a politician, but the sort who would run for city council in Youngstown on an antidevelopment, proecology ticket. He smiled too much. The Reverend Bumphead was a young man of Ichabod Crane lank. I never caught his denomination. My guess is Zen Methodist. He was either growing a beard or didn't know how to shave.

Mrs. Pigeon opened the proceedings in a patronizing tone that propelled me back through twenty-five years to the vile confines of the fourth grade. It was a beautiful afternoon, hot sun, clear sky, and just the right crisp breeze. The conference was being held on top of the cruise boat, but the 120 or so participants had jammed themselves in under the shade deck, where they were surrounded by superstructure on three sides and the air was stifling.

The peaceniks took notes. I had a vision of newsletters, reams and reams of misstapled copier paper Xeroxed when the boss wasn't looking, vomiting forth from the tepid organizations these people represented. "My Interesting Peace Voyage Through the Soviet Union"; "An Interesting and Enjoyable Visit to the USSR with Peace in Mind"; "Not *War and Peace* but *Peace and Peace*" (one of the clever ones); "Peace in the Soviet Union and an Interesting Trip There Too." Maybe America could be bored into nuclear disarmament.

Republican Party Reptile

Nick Smarm began to speak. It was the standard fare. He laid the greater part of the blame for a potential international nuke duke-out on the American doorstep. What he was saying wasn't wrong, at least not in the factual citations he made. But suddenly and quite against my will I was angry. To stand in front of strangers and run your country, *my* country, down—I didn't care if what Nick said was generally true, I didn't care if what he said was wholly, specifically, and exactly true in every detail. I haven't been that mad in years. I had to leave, go below. I was ashamed of the man. And it occurred to me that I would have been ashamed if he were Russian and we were on the Mississippi. That big fellow with the medals down his suit coat, my ally, he wouldn't have done such a thing on the *Delta Queen*.

I had a drink and went back. Reverend Bumphead from the Princeton Coalition for Disarmament was speaking now. He said exactly the same thing.

"Now it's time for all of us to ask Nick Smarm and Reverend Bumphead some interesting questions," said Mrs. Pigeon.

"Mr. Smarm," said a fat man, "now this is just a hypothetical question, but the way you were describing how the arms race is mostly the fault of the United States, couldn't I, if I were a red-baiter type, say—just hypothetically now—that you were a paid Soviet agent?" And he hastily added, "Please don't anybody take my question literally!" They took his question literally. The fat man was smothered in literalism. Squeals of indignation wafted toward the banks of the Don.

"What a terrible thing to say!" shrieked one of the leftist ladies. I'll bet she was pissed—all those friends of hers acting as Soviet agents for years, and no one ever offered to pay *them*.

I was about to put in a word for Pudgy, but it was too late. He was already overapologizing to Nick.

"What is the cost of housing in the Soviet Union as a percentage of worker wages?" asked a leftist. Reverend Bumphead didn't know the answer to that, so Mrs. Pigeon answered the rest of the questions.

P. J. O'Rourke

**VERY EARLY FRIDAY MORNING,
JULY 23**

I tried to explain my patriotic seizure to Nikolai. "Wouldn't you feel the same?" But I didn't seem to be getting through.

I gave up. We had more drinks. About twenty minutes later Nikolai said to me, "I did not think Nick's speech was so interesting." He pulled a deadpan face. *"I can read Pravda."*

FRIDAY, JULY 23

Ashore in Volgograd we were taken to Momayev Hill, where umpteen million people died defending the place when it was still named after Stalin. One of the leftists chaffed me for wearing a suit and tie again. I mean, we were going to visit a mass grave.

The leftists had their wreath, but watching them present it in their bowling shirts was more than I could bear. Besides, there was a fifty-two-meter-high statue of "Mother Russia" on top of the hill, and it's pretty interesting if you've never seen a reinforced-concrete nipple four feet across.

It wasn't until that afternoon, after four days on the boat, that I discovered there were real Americans aboard. Some ordinary tourists had stumbled into this morass of the painfully caring and hopelessly committed. By price or by accident they had picked this tour, and they were about as happy as if they'd signed up for a lemming migration.

When I came back from Momayev Hill, I saw a normal-looking, unagitated person stretched out on the sundeck in a T-shirt from Air America, the old CIA-run Southeast Asia airline. "What got you on this tour?" he asked, when I stared at the logo.

"I guess masochism," I said and looked again at the T-shirt.

He puffed out his chest. *"This* ought to shake the bastards up."

He was one of a dozen New Mexicans, all friends, traveling together on a private tour. Until now they'd had a wonderful time in the USSR. They said it was a fine place as long as you could drink like a Russian and leave like an American. But they'd taken this cruise without any idea of the peace that lay in store for them, and since they'd come on board they'd barricaded themselves in the promenade-deck lounge and had kept the leftists out with loud western accents and the peaceniks away by smoking cigarettes. Smoking cigarettes seems to alarm peace activists much more than voting for Reagan does.

The New Mexicans had become special pets of the barmaid. They were allowed to take glasses, ice, bottles, and china forward to the lounge. She wouldn't take tips from them, but Billy, a Santa Fe architect, had gone to the market in Rostov and brought the girl an armload of flowers. She blushed to the clavicle.

The New Mexicans were amazed at their fellow passengers, not in the matter of politics, but because the passengers were so rude to the crew. "And to each other," said Sue Ann, a real-estate developer. "I've never heard husbands and wives crap at each other like that in my life."

When it came to politics, Tom, a former AID officer with the State Department in Vietnam, said, "After all, there hasn't been a *great big war* since the A-bomb was invented."

"I live in Alamogordo," said Sue Ann. "I'll bet that shakes the bastards up." Indeed, that did bother some of the peaceniks, though the Air America T-shirt didn't—not one knew what it was.

SOVIET-AMERICAN RELATIONS IN ACTION

That evening at dinnertime, seven or eight young Russians from the local Soviet-American friendship club were ushered on board by Mrs. Pigeon. I noticed they gobbled the meat. Their president was a stiff young fellow, a future first secretary of the Committee for Lies About Grain Production if ever there was one. He had a guitar about two times bigger than normal and a watchful mien. But the others were okay. I sat between Alexei, a construction foreman who looked to be twelve, and Boris, an engineer (practically everyone in Russia is an engineer, just like our sanitation engineers are).

P. J. O'Rourke

Alexei wanted to talk about rock 'n' roll. His English was no worse than the average *Rolling Stone* reviewer's. "Abba—too nothing. Hard rock! Yay! Led Zeppelin! Yay! And Kiss!! I most like—hard, hard rock! You know of Time Machine?" He was very excited that an American recognized the name of the top Russian rock group. "Good like Beatles. But is best hard rock America, yay! Is only too bad always rock stars so many dying of too much liquor and"—he shot a glance at the president—"and of other things."

Boris wanted to talk about cars. In his opinion Russia needed much, much faster cars. "I want fast car," he said.

The Americans wanted to talk about peace and Soviet-American relations.

We went to the boat-deck music room after dinner with about ten Americans, mostly leftists, and Marya to help translate. There was one lady among the leftists I had not noticed before, though she was markedly ugly. It was not the kind of ugliness that's an accident of birth but the kind that is the result of years of ill temper, pique, and petty malice. These had given a rattish, shrewish, leaf-nosed-bat quality to her face.

The president said, "We are thankfully welcomed of being here. English ours is not so well. But is practicing now you with more." Then each of the Russian kids introduced himself and said his profession as best he could.

The ugly woman took aim at Alexei and said with great acerbity, "How many women construction workers are there in the Soviet Union?"

Alexei tried to answer. "Is construction worker training in mostly male, men I am meaning, but is also some girls if . . ." He got no further.

"Girls?!" shrieked the old bitch. *"Girls?!* We don't call *women* girls! That's an insult!" The Russian kids stared at her, mystified. The hag turned on Marya. "You explain to them that calling women girls is a demeaning thing to do."

Marya said something placating in Russian. The president tried a halting apology, but the ugly woman interrupted. "One

61

thing I'd like to know." She glared at Alexei's denim trousers. "Why do young people all over Europe, even in the socialist countries, pick up that awful American popular music and those sloppy blue jeans?"

Marya made what sounded like a pained verbatim translation. All the Russian faces in the room froze into the great Russian public face—serious but expressionless, part poker face and part the face the troops made on *You'll Never Get Rich*, when Phil Silvers asked for volunteers.

It isn't easy to get a sober Russian to do anything on impulse, but I took Marya by the cuff and convinced her we'd better get some beer from the bar. The room was still silent when we returned. The president wouldn't take a drink, but the rest of the Russians seemed glad enough to bury their faces in beer. The ugly woman sat smugly, still waiting for a reply. The other Americans were getting embarrassed. Finally, the woman's husband spoke up. He was wearing his running shorts and Kenneth Patchen T-shirt again. "What is the cost of housing in the Soviet Union as a . . ."

Something had to be done. I stood up. "I think it's very unfair for us to monopolize the comradeship and international goodwill of these Soviet young people," I said. "There is another group of Americans in the lounge who are eager to discuss Soviet-American relations with our guests, and—"

"Oh, yes!" said Marya, and she began to point to the hallway and chatter in Russian. The New Mexicans were a little surprised to see us, but their hospitality didn't falter.

"We are thankfully welcomed of being here," said the president. "English ours is not so—"

"The hell with that," said Tom. "Play us a song on that thing." And it was a pretty good song, and Sue Ann even got him to have a drink when he finished.

SATURDAY, JULY 24
There was another peace conference under the shade deck, and this time it was the Russians' turn to speak. I was slightly late, due to

sheer reluctance. Mrs. Pigeon was opening the session. "It is better to get these answers from Soviet experts than from our press," she was saying as I walked in. I walked back out again and had a beer. Actually, I had three.

When I returned, Guvov, the buffoon, had wound up his speech and was answering a question about whether Solzhenitsyn was just a bad writer or a spy too. He was wearing a hilarious pair of ersatz Levi's with TEXAS JEAN printed on a salad-plate-sized plastic patch on the ass. "Solzhenitsyn painted the Soviet Union only in dark colors," he said. The leftists clapped vigorously. "Criticism," said Guvov, "leads to the problems of democracy."

Time for more beer.

It seemed to be dawning on a few of the peaceniks that something was askew. When I returned from the bar the second time, one of them was addressing Guvov. "A lot of the Americans on this trip have admitted the errors of American foreign policy. How come none of the Soviets have admitted any Soviet errors?"

"We don't criticize the foreign policy of our government," said Guvov, "because we hundred-percent agree with it and approve of it." The questioner gasped. But the leftists all clapped, and so did quite a few of the peaceniks.

That was it for me and peace conferences. I apologize, but this reporter did not attend any more peace functions of any kind.

LOATH BOAT

The leftists and peaceniks spent most of every day talking. They were not arguing. They were not analyzing. They were not making observations. What they were doing was agreeing with each other —in feverish spasms of accordance, mad confabs of apposition, blathers of consonance. On Reagan, on the weapons freeze, on the badness of Israel, on the dangers of war, on the need for peace, they agreed.

I finally decided these people were crazy.

I watched my cabin mate write a letter to his wife. It was a political exhortation. "We Americans must repudiate the Reagan administration . . ." This to his wife of thirty years.

Crazy. And stupid too.

One, who was from the deep Midwest and looked like Millicent Fenwick, told me, "You know, if the people who put Reagan in office prevail, they're going to take the vote from women."

As we were going through the locks of the Don-Volga canal the woman with the direct connection between her cerebral cortex and her mouth came nattering up beside me at the rail. "Isn't it marvelous?" she said, staring at a gigantic blank wall of concrete. "They're such wonderful engineers in the Soviet Union." I agreed it was an impressive piece of work. "Marvelous, marvelous, marvelous, marvelous," she said. She peeked over the side. "And where *do* they get all the water?"

The Intourist guides were at wits' end, the Soviet experts were becoming testy, and the crew was clearly disgusted and getting into the grog ration earlier each day.

The ship's doctor, a blowsy, mottle-eyed, disbarred-looking fellow, had taken to experimenting on the diarrhea symptoms half the Americans were suffering. Marya gave an elaborate burlesque of accompanying him as the translator on his rounds. The Russians would not explain the joke, but I know one peacenik had gone to him with the malady and received a laxative and a glass of 200-proof neutral grain spirits. I did not see that person again for thirty-six hours.

SUNDAY, JULY 25
Sunday I was drunk.

P. J. O'Rourke

WHAT WAS GOING ON IN THE SOVIET CAPITAL AND HEARTLAND AS WE JOINED *THE NATION* THIS SUMMER ON AN EXCITING AND AFFORDABLE SOVIET EXCURSION?

I know I'll never understand what the Americans thought they were doing in Russia, but I'm almost as confused about what the Russians thought they were letting them do.

Obviously the Volga Peace Cruise was approved. Unapproved things unhappen in the USSR. But though the Soviets had approved it, they didn't seem very interested. In one of the cities where we docked, a local reporter came aboard and talked to Nick Smarm. When Nick finished excoriating the U.S. and began pointing out that the Soviet Union was also engaged in the arms race, the reporter simply stopped writing. This was the total media attention given us.

I suppose we were under surveillance. I noticed that Sonya took complete notes during the conferences, but it seemed to me she was paying most attention to what her countrymen said. Some peaceniks suspected their rooms had been searched. One woman had found her bags a little too neatly closed and zipped. Another woman had her copy of *Peter the Great* disappear.

"Do not bother to look for it," said one of the Intourist guides, when the woman made a stink. "It has doubtless slipped behind the folding bunk when the steward lady has been making the bed. It is most difficult to look under there so steward lady will do it for you during dinner." This sounded suspicious. But the book did not mysteriously reappear after dinner, not even with certain pages torn out, so maybe it was just lost.

Neither I nor the outspokenly pro-American New Mexicans were bothered. One day Nikolai and Sonya took me on a nice but pointless speedboat ride up the Volga, and I assumed this was when my cabin was to be searched. But I'd used the old Ian Fleming trick of fastening a human hair with spit across my locker door and it was still there when I got back.

If anything was happening to the leftists, they weren't talking. But one of them, the woman who was embarrassed to have left the Soviet Union as a child, had relatives in Moscow, whom I know she visited. When we went through customs at the end of the tour, she was searched completely and questioned so long that the plane had to be held for her. Our tour leader claimed it was because she'd lost one of her currency exchange receipts.

Whatever the official Soviet attitude toward us may have been, the private Russian attitude was manifestly clear. The Russians, when they'd had a few drinks, would repeatedly make declarations starting, "I am not an anti-Semite, but . . ." And, at least to judge by last names, many of our tour members were Jewish.

One of the crew, in the most confidence-imparting stage of drunkenness, told me, "You know Brezhnev is married to a Jew. Many members of the Presidium are married to Jews. This is why we cannot be so firm with the Israelis."

But the peaceniks and the leftists were blind to this, or passed it off as anti-Zionism only. Their only serious concern was with the CIA. They were convinced there must be a CIA agent aboard. I suggested the fat man, surely an agent provocateur. But they'd decided he was okay, since he'd apologized to Nick. Someone said the leftists suspected me—that coat and tie. I asked Nikolai who he thought it was. "All of them," he laughed.

MONDAY, JULY 26
I think the Russians had decided both privately and officially that these Volga peace cruisers were inconsequential people, unable to influence American policy in any important way.

When we docked in Togliatti, the leftists were very eager to see the Lada automobile plant there, one of the most modern factories in the Soviet Union. They were swooning to meet genuine "workers." But it wasn't on the schedule. Our Intourist guides made a halfhearted attempt to convince the local Intourist office to allow a tour, but it was too big a group, too many officials would have to be contacted, it would take too long to arrange, and so on. The leftists were pretty sore, and went so far as to make no excuses for the Soviet system this time.

But meanwhile Nikolai had somehow got in touch with the Lada plant management and informed them that I worked for *Car and Driver* magazine. I'm only a contributing editor there, and even if I were editor in chief I wouldn't have much sway over the FTC, DOT, and Reagan administration executive orders that keep the Russians from exporting cars to us. But I was a representative of the real world nonetheless. And that afternoon there was a big chauffeured car waiting at dockside to take me, the only admitted Republican on board, for a personal tour of the Lada plant.

ALL THE REST OF THE DAYS ON THE TRIP

By Tuesday the 27th I'd come to the end of the tour, at least as a sentient being. There were still two days left to the cruise and six days left in Russia, but I was gone.

The place just wears you out after a while. There is not a square angle or a plumb line in all the country. Every bit of concrete is crumbling from too much aggregate in the mix, and *everything* is made of concrete. I saw buildings with the facades falling off that were still under construction. And everything that's well built turns out to be built by somebody else. Moscow Airport was built by West Germans, the Grand Hyatt knockoff by the French, the Lada plant by Italians, the very boat was made in Austria.

The air pollution in the cities is grotesque. No machine seems to run well. And the whole of commerce visible on the Volga consisted of carting sand and phone poles from one port to the next.

The New Mexicans had a contest: a bottle of champagne to be won by the first person who saw a crane with an operator in it. No one won. Every building site we saw was three-fourths deserted. I asked Orlonsky where the workers were, but he turned sly on me. "Perhaps they are at lunch." It was 10:30 in the morning.

What little of the old and charming architecture is left is rotting, sitting neglected, waiting to be torn down for its lack of modernism. Russia stinks of dirty bodies and evil Balkan tobacco and a disinfectant they must distribute by the tank car daily, some chemical with a moldy turned-earth stench as though vandals had been at it in the graveyard or mice had gotten into the mushroom cellar.

In the end, every little detail starts to get to you—the overwhelming oppressiveness of the place, the plain godawfulness of it.

We put in at Ulyanovsk, birthplace of Lenin. Not an easy city to find your way around in. Take Lenin Avenue to Lenin Street; go straight to Lenin Square, then left along Lenin Boulevard to Lenin Place and Lenin Lane. Don't miss the monument to Lenin's sister's dog.

And there's no reason to find your way around. There's nothing there, anyway. We were shitfaced drunk in the bar by noon. The New Mexicans and I were crazed now with the desire for a cheeseburger, mad for the sound of a pedal steel guitar, would have killed for a six-pack of Budweiser and a ride down the interstate at 100 miles an hour in a Cadillac Coupe de Ville. But there was nothing to be done, nothing to do but drink. So we drank and told jokes: old jokes, bad jokes, dirty jokes.

We were interrupting the progressives' dinner now. The leftists and the peaceniks were mad. But only Mrs. Pigeon had the courage to approach. What were we laughing about?

"Sex," said Sue Ann.

"Now, what's so funny about sex?" said Mrs. Pigeon.

"Well, if you don't remember, honey . . ." And Mrs. Pigeon retreated. We began to sing. We sang "Silver Threads and Golden Needles" and "Danny Boy" and:

P. J. O'Rourke

My mother sells rubbers to sailors,
My dad pokes the heads with a pin,
My sister performs the abortions,
My God how the money rolls in.

The progressives could not get the Russians to stop us. Instead, the Russians came back from the fantail and began to sing too, loud Russian songs with stamping and pounding of glasses. Then some of the peaceniks came up and then a few more, and they began to sing along. They sang "America the Beautiful" and "God Bless America" and every verse to "The Star Spangled Banner," a most cacophonous sound. We danced, and the ship's band tried to play jitterbug. And the Russians gave toasts, and we gave toasts:

> *To the American Eagle,*
> *The higher she goes, the louder she screams,*
> *And who fucks with the eagle best learn how to fly!*

And the Russians said:

> *To Mother Russia,*
> *Who comes here with the sword*
> *Dies by the sword!*

And someone said, "From one bunch of sons of a bitches to another." And we drank everything that came to hand, the doctor's neutral grain spirits included, and sang and danced and drank some more until we passed out on top of the tables in a triumph of peace and Soviet-American relations.

There's nothing at all to the rest of the trip except a huge gray-and-green hangover with a glimpse of the White Kremlin making my head ache in Kazan and the band piping us ashore in the morning with, most appropriately to my mind, "The Battle

Hymn of the Republic." Then a flight to Moscow, rough weather all the way, and back to that Grand Hyatt hotel.

There was a Russian disco band in the lounge, balalaika music played on electric guitars and set to a Donna Summer beat. The New Mexicans went on to Leningrad, and I was left sitting alone in the bar waiting for my plane home a day and a half hence. An English tourist sat down next to me. "Been here long, have you?" he said. "Been all around the country?"

"I've been to the fucking back of the moon!" I said. "Scotch," I said to the bartender. He gave me vodka.

Goons, Guns, and Gold

~~~~~~

On the day before the 1986 Philippine presidential election, a Manila bartender tells me this one: President Marcos and General Ver find themselves in hell. General Ver is up to his neck in boiling tar. President Marcos is up to his knees. General Ver says: "Look, I've been your right-hand man for twenty years, and I've done some terrible stuff, but it's nothing compared to what you've done. How come you're only up to your knees?"

President Marcos says, "I'm standing on Imelda's shoulders."

A taxi driver tells me this one: Imelda and her kids, Irene, Imee, and Bongbong (this is, no kidding, what Marcos's twenty-seven-year-old son, Ferdinand Jr., is called), are flying over the Philippines in their jet. Irene says: "Mommy, the Philippine people really hate us. Isn't there something we can do?"

"I've got an idea," says Bongbong. "We'll drop ten thousand

packages out of the airplane. Each package will have fifty pesos in it. The people can buy rice and fish, and they'll love us."

"I've got a better idea," says Imee. "We'll only drop five thousand packages out of the airplane. But each package will have one hundred pesos in it. The people can buy chicken and pork, and they'll love us even more."

"I've got the best idea," says Imelda. "We'll drop just one package out of the airplane, and the people will love us forever."

"What's in that package, Mom?" say the kids.

"Your father."

In Tondo, Manila's largest slum, I see a cigarette boy with a picture of President Marcos on the front of his vending tray. My companion, who speaks Tagalog, the local dialect, asks him, "Why do you have a picture of Marcos there?"

The boy runs his thumbnail across the president's profile and says, "I like to scratch his face off."

In a bar on Pilar Street, in the red-light district, some fellow journalists and I are surrounded by B-girls. Liquor cannot be served to Filipinos the night before an election, and the place is dead. A dozen smooth-skinned, peanut-butter-colored girls in tiny white bikinis are rubbing against us like kittens. Somebody orders them a round of $5 orange juices. In an attempt to somehow get this on my expense account, I ask, "Who are you going to vote for?" The girls make an L sign, thumb out, index finger up. It's the symbol of UNIDO/PDP-LABAN, the coalition backing Corazon Aquino.

My favorite B-girl, Jolly, who has the face of a pouty Hawaiian beauty queen and a body that could cause sins of commission at a hundred yards, takes a playful punch at my nose. *"Laban!"* she says. It means "struggle" in Tagalog. "I vote for Cory."

The other girls giggle. "She's not old enough to vote," says one.

"We're all for Cory," says another. "Even the mama-sans are for Cory." The mama-sans are the combination madams and bunny mothers of these establishments. They hire the girls, make sure you buy drinks, and charge you a "bar fine" if you take anybody home. I ask a mama-san, and she agrees. "Everybody here is for Cory. Only owners are for Marcos."

And I wouldn't be so sure about that. I visit an owner, an Aussie thug who runs one of the B-girl joints on Pilar Street. He's about forty, blond, thick-chested, with mean blue eyes and an accent as broad as the space I'd give him if he were swinging a chair in a bar fight. His office is a windowless upstairs room. The desk is covered with thousands of pesos, bundled in rubber bands.

"The tourist trade has gone to hell," says the Aussie. "And it'll get worse with all the crap you reporters are turning out about the election. But something's got to be done for the Flips, doesn't it? They can only take so much, can't they? Now they'll be up in the hills with the New People's Army or some bloody thing."

Thugs, whores, cabbies, street Arabs, gin jockeys—these are by nature conservative folk. When you lose this bunch, your ass is oatmeal. You'd better pack your Dictator-model Vuitton bags and pray the U.S. Air Force will Baby Doc you someplace nice.

To think that they had an "election contest" in the Philippines is to get it all wrong. It was a national upchuck. It was everybody with sense or scruples versus everybody corrupt, frightened, or mindlessly loyal.

Marcos, like any good crime boss, knew how to command loyalty. He co-opted the two traditional political parties and formed them into his own nonideological New Society Party, the KBL. He declared martial law to avoid giving up office in 1972 and then changed the constitution so he could rule by decree and be reelected in perpetuity. He sent hit men after some of his enemies, jailed others, and forced the rest into exile. Then he ruined the Philippine economy by granting monopolies on everything from sugar milling and copra processing to grain importing and by pumping oceans of government money into lame and corrupt corporations—a system known as crony capitalism.

According to *Newsweek*, American and Philippine economists estimate that Marcos and pals shipped as much as $20 billion out of the country. We're not talking about Michèle Duvalier's fur collection. Twenty billion dollars is more than half the Philippine gross national product, enough money to turn the archipelago into Hong Kong II. By comparison, total U.S. aid to the Philippines since independence in 1946 has been less than $4 billion.

Reporters who do duty in the third world spend a lot of time saying, "It's not that simple." We say, "It's not that simple about the Israelis and the PLO," or "It's not that simple about the contras and the Sandinistas." But in the Philippines it was that simple. It was simpler than that. Ferdinand Marcos is human sewage, an evil old power-addled flaming Glad Bag, a vicious lying dirtball who ought to have been dragged through the streets of Manila with his ears nailed to a truck bumper.

GOONS, GUNS, AND GOLD

As a traditional phrase describing Philippine elections, "goons, guns, and gold" doesn't cover it. I know everyone has heard this election was stolen. But, Jesus, the cheek of the thing. The fix was more obvious than a skit on this season's *Saturday Night Live*.

Marcos had complete control of Philippine television. On Manila's Channel 4, the anchorman was a smirking toadeater named Ronnie Nathanialz—in looks and delivery, a sort of Don Ho from hell. He was known locally as TV Ronnie Sip-Sip Tuta. In Tagalog, *tuta* means "puppy" or "lap dog," and *sip-sip* is something worse than ass kissing. TV Ronnie's news broadcast would go: "Good evening, viewers, and welcome to popular Channel 4 news. Tonight we continue our unbiased coverage of the honest, fair, and peaceful Philippine elections where much-admired President Ferdinand E. Marcos is showing a commanding lead according to all reliable commentators."

I'm not making this up. If you listened to Channel 4 for more than a minute, you'd start boxing yourself on the ears, trying to get the steady hum of bullshit out of your head.

Then Channel 4 would broadcast a taped segment from COMELEC, the government election commission. Functionaries would hold an empty ballot box up to the camera ("Nothing in the hat!"), then show all the locks and seals to be attached to each box and demonstrate how this box would be carefully moved under military guard from hither to thither, and so forth. It looked like the election was being fixed by a high school magic club.

On election day, between seven hundred and a thousand foreign reporters spread across the country watching voter-registration records being destroyed, ballot boxes stolen, opposition poll watchers barred from their stations, and army trucks full of "flying voters" moved from one polling spot to another. Marcos was doing everything but training circus animals to vote.

About half an hour before the polls closed, I had my driver take me to his precinct so he could cast his ballot. It was a comfortable middle-class neighborhood called Bay Palms. The polling place was a tidy scene, voters standing neatly in line, ballot boxes screened for privacy. A quietly enthusiastic crowd of Aquino supporters was gathered at the proper legal distance from the polls.

And the military was right in the middle of it, a full company, armed, with a general standing on a truck screeching through a bullhorn. Volunteers from NAMFREL, the National Movement for Free Elections, were nearly in tears.

"What's going on?" I asked.

"The military is here to close the polls exactly on the hour," said a matronly woman, "even though the people waiting in line to vote are supposed to be able to do so as long as they were in line before three o'clock."

"I don't understand."

"Bay Palms is an anti-Marcos district," she said. "And in the next district, Guadalupe, only a mile away, our volunteers are calling for help. There is violence and thugs and the ballot boxes are being stolen, and we have begged the military to go stop the violence in Guadalupe, but they are here making sure this polling place closes on time instead."

My driver came back. "I can't vote," he said. "They're making sure the polling place closes on time."

I went back to the hotel and ordered a drink. A moment later an Australian television crew came running into the bar, their eyes as big as pie plates. "In Guadalupe," one yelled, "there's violence and thugs and the ballot boxes are being stolen!"

"And they *shot* at us," yelled another, "and took our camera at gunpoint and smashed it and grabbed the videotape!"

The Australians, being as dumb as Australians, called the police. In a little while there were a couple of greasy Criminal Investigation Service agents in the bar, drinking it up on the Aussies' tab and hinting broadly that for 10,000 pesos maybe the videotape could be found, but probably not until after the election.

I went up to my room, hoping that I had some drugs I'd forgotten about in my luggage. TV Ronnie was on the air with the Metro Manila chief of police. "Yes," said the chief, "there have been no reports of election-related trouble in the Metro Manila region."

A SALVAGE HIT

"The election was marred by violence" is a nice phrase. It summons images of teens with cans of aerosol mayhem, going out to deface campaign posters. Photographer Tony Suau and I went to investigate one such mar or scuff near the town of Moncada, in Tarlac province, about 130 kilometers north of Manila.

Political killing in the Philippines is called "salvaging"—the victim has been "salvaged from communism." This was not one of the big murders that made headlines in the United States or even in Manila. The opposition papers gave it one paragraph and spelled the man's name wrong. He was Arsenio Cainglet, a tenant farmer in a rural barangay called Banquero Sur.

Arsenio was the barangay captain for the UNIDO opposition party. We had to drive a long way from the paved road to find his house, through miles of flat rice land tufted with stands of bamboo and coconut palms, looking everything like snapshots my drafted buddies brought back from Vietnam. At a hut that serves as the Banquero Sur town hall and medical center I found two members of the CHDF, the Civil Home Defense Force, which is supposed to be for anti-guerrilla self-defense but has been used more often as a local enforcement arm of the KBL. This pair looked like somebody gave the town drunks M-16s. They were surly but seemed frightened by Tony's cameras. A touching omniscience and potency was being attributed to the foreign press just then. And not many people with blue eyes ever venture to Banquero Sur anyway. They gave us directions to Arsenio's home.

Several dozen mournful people stood in the yard. Fifty feet away were three uniformed policemen surrounding a fat-necked man in civilian clothes. "Please don't use my name," said Agent Ramos of the Criminal Investigation Service. He wore a large gold ring and gold Rolex and reported no progress on the case. "Mayor Llamas is investigating," he said, pointing to a thin chain-smoking man of about sixty talking to the people in the yard. The moment I turned my back, Agent Ramos and his policemen slipped away.

Rodolfo D. Llamas is actually the ex-mayor, and not of Moncada but of the next town down the road, Paniqui. He was there because he's the UNIDO District Coordinator.

At sunrise on the previous day Arsenio Cainglet was sitting in front of his house holding his favorite fighting cock. A man in civilian clothes drove up. The villagers described him as "with a big hat, big jacket." He shot Arsenio five times with a .45 automatic. Arsenio said, "Bakit?"—"Why?"—and fell dead on the spot. He was forty-three years old and had nine children, ages one to eighteen.

"Arsenio was looking for me a couple of days ago," said Llamas, "but I was in Manila on election business. I would have gotten him to a safe house if I had known in time." He said he'd given money to his own family and sent them out of town. "I go home by the back way."

The Cainglet house was made of nailed and lashed bamboo and set on stilts. Its two rooms were reached by walking carefully up a set of steep bamboo-log rungs. I could feel the structure sway from our weight. They'd brought the coffin up there somehow, a crude but elaborately carved and gilded casket with a glass cover, like a reliquary's, over the open top half. Arsenio's mother, a tiny old woman, was trying to embrace the whole box, wailing and rubbing her forehead on the glass. The corpse was fierce, Mexican-looking—black hair combed straight back and dead features set in an angry frown no American mortician could have accomplished.

"The KBL was trying to turn him," said Llamas, "get him to change sides, but he wouldn't go along."

Sunlight shone into the little house through the walls and even the floor. A modest buffet had been laid out for the mourners on a table beside the household altar. Arsenio's widow showed me, in the palm of her hand, one of the .45 slugs that had been dug out of his body. She had an expression on her face I don't think we have in our culture, a kind of smile of hatred.

Cory Aquino didn't even carry the barangay. The vote had been Aquino 99, Marcos 206. I asked the people in the house—the eldest daughter, who'd been to high school, translating—if this reflected the political feelings of the village. There was an audible collective snort. The mourners looked startled. Some of them laughed. Then they were silent.

"They don't want to talk," the daughter said. "They're scared."

When I came outside Llamas hinted I might escort him back to the paved road. He was traveling with four bodyguards.

FOUR HUNDRED YEARS IN A CONVENT, FIFTY YEARS IN A WHOREHOUSE

Spain owned the Philippines from 1521 to 1898, and America from 1898 to 1946. Pundits summarize this history as "four hundred years in a convent, fifty years in a whorehouse." Manila today looks like some Ancient Mariner who has lived through it all. The boulevards are tattered and grim and overhung with a dirty hairnet of electrical and phone wires. The standard-issue third-world concrete buildings are stained dead-meat gray by the emphysematous air pollution. Street lighting is haphazard. Ditto for street cleaning. The streets themselves are filled with great big holes. Fires seem to be frequent. Visits from the fire department less so. There are numerous burned-out buildings. Every now and then you see what must have been charming Old Manila architecture—tin-roofed houses with upper stories that jut over the streets and windows boxed by trelliswork. Now these houses sag and flop. They don't seem to have been painted since the Japanese occupation. In fact, the first impression of Manila is of a defeated city, still occupied and exploited by some hostile force. Which has been more or less the case—Imelda Marcos was governor of the Metro Manila region for the past decade. You see her handiwork in occasional pieces of huge, brutish modernism rising uninvited from Manila's exhausted clutter. There is, for instance, the Cultural Center Complex, plopped on some landfill disfiguring Manila Bay. One of its buildings is the Manila Film Center, which Imelda rushed to completion in time for a 1982 international film festival. The story goes that the hurriedly poured concrete roof collapsed, burying forty or more workers in wet cement. No attempt was made to rescue them. This would have meant missing the deadline. The floor was laid over their corpses. Supposedly, Imelda later held an exorcism to get rid of the building's malevolent ghosts.

During the election, standard journalistic practice was to go to Forbes Park in the Manila suburbs, where Marcos's cronies were wallowing in money, then make a quick dash to the downtown slums—"Manila: City of Contrasts." Tony Suau was shooting a polo match in Forbes Park when one of the players trotted over between chukkers and said, "Going to Tondo next, huh?"

I visited one pretty rough place myself. It was occupied almost entirely by gang members, teenage boys with giant tattoos over their arms, legs, backs, and I don't know where else. The gangs have names like Sigue-Sigue Sputnik and Bahala Na Gang. (*Sigue-sigue* means "go-go"; *bahala na* means "I don't care.") Members slash themselves on the chest to make ritual scars, one for every person they've killed. Each gang's turf is blocked off, with one or more kids guarding the entrance with clubs.

Actually, things were pretty clean around there. Nice vivid religious murals had been painted on the walls. Fishponds had been dug and vegetable gardens planted for the residents.

What I'm describing, however, is the Manila city jail. It's a relaxed place where friends and family come and visit all day. There are no cells, just long barracks where prisoners sleep on low wooden platforms. If they like, they can build their own tiny huts.

Hard to know what to say about a country where the only decent low-income housing is in the hoosegow.

The warden, a cheerful stomachy man, greeted me in his office while he pulled on his Adidas sweatpants. He was the only solid Marcos supporter I met. "What an open, free society to have such democratic debate," said the warden about the elections. I complimented him on his jail. He bought me a Sprite.

The real slums are another matter. The bad parts of Tondo are as bad as any place I've seen, ancient, filthy houses swarmed with the poor and stinking of sewage and trash. But there are worse parts—squatter areas where people live under cardboard, in shipping crates, behind tacked-up newspapers. Dad would march you straight to the basement with a hairbrush in his hand if he caught you keeping your hamster cage like this.

The world's a shocking poor place and probably always has been. I think I'm no hairless innocent about this. But the Philippines is an English-speaking nation with an 89 percent literacy rate. It has land, resources, and an educated middle class. It has excellent access to American markets, and it's smack on the Pacific Rim, the only economic boom region in the world right now. It used to have one of the highest standards of living in Asia. There can't be any excuse for this.

P. J. O'Rourke

~~~~~~

And when you think you may actually get sick from what you've seen, you come to Smoky Mountain.

This is the main Manila trash dump, a vast fifty-foot hill of smoldering garbage, and in that garbage people are living—old people, pregnant women, little babies. There is a whole village of dirty hovels, of lean-tos and pieces of sheltering junk planted in the excrement and muck. These loathsome homes are so thickly placed I could barely make my way between them. The path in some places was not a foot wide, and I sank to my ankles in the filth.

People are eating the offal from this dung heap, drinking and washing in the rivulets of water that run through it. There are children with oozing sores, old people with ulcer-eaten eyes, crippled men lying in the waste. They live worse than carrion birds, pulling together bits of old plastic to sell. There's not much else of value in the rubbish. Not even the good garbage gets to these people.

In Smoky Mountain you don't feel disgust or nausea, just cold shock. I looked up and saw an immense whirlwind of detritus spiraling away from the dump's crest, something that would take a malnourished Dorothy off to the Dirt Oz.

I went back to the hotel and put on a pair of Bass Weejuns. I'd been told that Imelda wouldn't let anyone into the presidential palace in rubber-soled shoes. She is reputedly as crazy as a rat in a coffee can, and the statuary on the palace grounds bore that out. It looked like she had broken into a Mexican birdbath factory.

You got a whiff around Malacanang Palace that you were dealing with people a few bricks shy of a load. At the gate, there was intense inspection of footwear and pocket tape recorders. I had a borrowed press ID with Tony's Suau's picture on it hanging around my neck. Tony and I look about as much alike as Moe and Curly, but this bothered the guards not at all.

The reception hall had obviously been decorated by a Las Vegas interior designer forced to lower his standards of taste at gunpoint. I mean, it had a parquet *ceiling*. There were red plush curtains and a red plush carpet and red plush upholstery on gold-leaf fake-bamboo chairs. The chandeliers were the size of parade floats, all wood, hand-carved, and badly too. And the air conditioning wasn't working.

It was the day after the election, and President Marcos was holding a press conference. It was completely uninteresting to see him in person. His puffy face was opaque. There was something of Nixon to his look, but not quite as nervous, and something of Mao, but not quite as dead. Marcos predicted how much he'd win by, which turned out to be how much he won by after his KBL-dominated legislature tallied the count. He blandly lied away, accusing the press of making things up and the other side of threats and cheating. One member of the press asked him about threats and cheating of his own. Said Marcos, "Why hasn't the opposition brought this to the attention of the authorities?" (Which were him.)

A reporter from the pro-Aquino *Manila Times* asked, "What will happen if there's no agreement about who won the election?"

"What do you think will happen?" said Marcos. For just a moment I thought that he wasn't making a threat, that he really didn't know.

I dozed in my fake-bamboo chair and was startled awake at the end of the session by Marcos saying, "When you see a nun touch a ballot box, that's an illegal act."

The stuff of nightmares, this country. And as every horror-movie director knows, it takes an element of the friendly and familiar to make a real nightmare. It has to be *Mom* eating snakes in the rec room.

In the Philippines, the element of the friendly and familiar is the Filipinos, remarkably nice people, cheerful, hospitable, unfailingly polite. Even the riot police and Marcos thugs were courteous when not actually terrorizing somebody. The gang members smile at you in jail. The dying smile at you in Smoky Mountain. When you ask a cab driver what the fare is, he says, "Ikaw ang bahala"—"It's up to you." In the worst red-light dive the atmosphere is like a Rotary lunch.

There was an anti-imperialist demonstration in front of our embassy. One of the protesters came up to Betsy West, an ABC-TV

^^^

Nightline producer, and said, "If you could please wait five minutes, we'll burn the American flag."

WHITE MONKEYS

^^^

For comic relief there was the U.S. Congressional observer team.

Its chairman, Indiana senator Richard Lugar, started out with his foot in his mouth down to the knee. Reporters called him the Stepford Senator because of his jerky physical motions and mechanical responses. After a couple of hours of cursory poll watching on election morning, Lugar told Manila's Channel 4 that everything seemed to be going along fine and "the only problems I saw were minor and technical." Channel 4 played this tape over and over again for the rest of the day. Early the next morning, Lugar was huffing with indignation and told Tom Brokaw, "It's a very, very suspicious count." But that didn't get local coverage.

Representative John Murtha, from Pennsylvania, was an improvement, at least in person. I ran into this big side of beef of a guy during the vote count at the city hall in Pasay, a working-class Manila suburb. He tried to make some statesmanlike noises about "the passionate commitment of the Philippine people to democracy," a phrase reporters were by then condensing to "Pash Commit of Flips to Dem." But outrage overtook him. "You can see what's going on!" he blurted. "You can see what the will of the people is!" And he said journalists should quit going to the same places he was and get out to as many vote-counting centers as they could. "You're the only hope," he said. (Which I've never been called by a politician, or anybody else for that matter.)

Most of the Potomac Parakeets were a big disappointment. Massachusetts senator John Kerry was a founding member of the Vietnam Veterans Against the War, but he was a bath toy in this fray.

On Sunday night, two days after the election, thirty of the computer operators from COMELEC walked off the job, protesting that vote figures were being juggled. Aquino supporters and NAM-FREL volunteers took the operators, most of them young women, to a church, and hundreds of people formed a protective barrier around them.

Village Voice reporter Joe Conason and I had been tipped off about the walkout, and when we got to the church, we found Bea Zobel, one of Cory Aquino's top aides, in a tizzy. "The women are terrified," she said. "They're scared to go home. They don't know what to do. We don't know what to do." Joe and I suggested that Mrs. Zobel go to the Manila Hotel and bring back some members of the Congressional observer team. She came back with Kerry, who did nothing.

Kerry later said that he didn't talk to the COMELEC employees then because he wasn't allowed to. This is ridiculous. He was ushered into an area that had been cordoned off from the press and the crowd and where the computer operators were sitting. To talk to the women, all he would have had to do was raise his voice. Why he was reluctant, I can't tell you. I can tell you what any red-blooded representative of the U.S. government should have done. He should have shouted, "If you're frightened for your safety, I'll take you to the American embassy, and damn the man who tries to stop me." But all Kerry did was walk around like a male model in a concerned and thoughtful pose.

Before the Congressional observer team went home, Lugar read a thin-soup statement, crinkum-crankum so packed with "Pash Commit of Flips to Dem" that a Hong Kong TV correspondent was moved to ask, "For those of us who are not native English speakers, could you please tell us what you're saying?" These guys may have talked tough stateside, but they had their mouths in the Delphic mush bowl when it counted.

Now they're giving each other bipartisan backslaps for their brilliant handling of a delicate foreign-policy crisis. But all the Filipinos saw was three weeks of President Reagan taking every position on the opinion compass about whether Marcos was a cool dude or what. The administration didn't get around to "throw the bum out" until Ferdinand and Imelda were practically unpacking their underwear in Guam. I don't think there's a way to exaggerate the true love we could have had in the Philippines if we'd gotten on the side of the angels and stayed there. But, I was quick to point out to my Philippine friends, it could have been worse. We could have lent B-52s to Marcos the way we did to Nguyen Van Thieu.

DOWN FOR THE COUNT

First thing in the morning on the day after the election, Tony Suau and I went to watch votes being counted at the city hall in Makati, Manila's central business district. It was clear, even before the polls closed, that Marcos would have to cheat before, during, and after the balloting. Cory Aquino had shaken up a warm six-pack of indignation, and the pop tops were off.

The ballot boxes, aluminum cubes about the size of milk crates, had been brought from Makati's polling places and stored in a warehouse behind the city hall. A couple thousand Aquino supporters surrounded the two buildings. The NAMFREL volunteers linked arms and formed a human corridor from the warehouse, across a plaza, through the city hall basement, up three flights of stairs, and down a hall to an assembly room. Every ballot box was carried through this double file by a flying wedge of a half-dozen people, each keeping at least one hand on that box.

Tony and I were on the second floor with one flying wedge that had obligingly stopped in midrun so we could interview them. Then we heard screaming and yelling in the lobby below.

One of the city hall policemen had taken issue with the NAMFREL human chain, a shoving match had followed, and a teenage girl had been thumped on the head.

The crowd went wild. Tony and I came downstairs just in time to get caught at the front of this nascent riot and squashed against the lobby's inner doors, which had been barred by retreating police. The crowd fell back to make a second rush, and the policemen came charging out. A club went whistling under my nose. Tony got truncheoned on the shoulder.

This was great! Just like taking over the dean's office in the sixties. It was all I could do to keep from leaping on a drinking fountain and screaming, "Stop the war!" A pretty inappropriate sentiment, since this wasn't a war and if it had been the crowd would have been all for it.

The police charged again, acting fairly restrained, if I have to tell the truth. Mostly they rushed at the mob with cross-body blocks and only used a little bit of clubbing every now and then. I looked over and saw Tony being shoved back by four or five policemen while behind him a dozen members of the crowd were pushing him forward, yelling: "Foreign press! Cover this!"

Eventually a NAMFREL leader, a police sergeant, and a Makati vice-mayor appeared with bullhorns and got everything settled down. The police would promise to stop hitting people if people would promise not to block public employees from going about their business, although it was Saturday and the only public employees going about their business were police.

Peace lasted five minutes. Tony and I were in the lobby with some policemen and some Aquino supporters who had obligingly stopped hollering at each other so we could interview them. Then we heard screaming and yelling at the back of the building.

A Mercedes had tried to pull into the city hall parking lot.

The crowd went wild. First they blocked its entry. Then the driver tried to leave. Then they blocked its exit. The police finally had to wade in and collect the car's two occupants and hustle them into the city hall.

"Who was in the car?" I shouted to the crowd.

"We don't know."

This sounded pretty dopey.

"No, no," yelled the crowd. "Maybe they are delivering something!" "It looked like envelopes!" "Envelopes the size of vote-tally sheets!"

"They are delivering fake vote-tally sheets!" the crowd concluded triumphantly and began rocking the car back and forth.

I went over and pressed my nose against the tinted windows. Inside, on the floor, were a pair of M-16 rifles. Whoever these guys were, they probably weren't goodwill ambassadors from the Little Sisters of the Poor. The police hustled them back out of the building and into the Mercedes. I never got a good look at the pair. The crowd pressed on the car. The driver pressed on the accelerator. The crowd began pounding on the fenders and hood. The police began pounding on the crowd. Somebody's head got busted and blood ran down his face. For a moment it was a standoff, but horsepower won out. Somehow no one was smeared under the wheels. The car tore through the crowd. People were heaved right and left. They picked themselves up and took off after the Mercedes, throwing stones and chunks of Manila's crummy pavement. These folks were worked up.

That night I went to the hip café in Manila, the Hobbit House, to see Freddie Aguilar, who's billed as "the Bob Dylan of the Philippines." This is unfair, since he's good-looking, plays the guitar well, can carry a tune, and writes songs that make sense.

Many of the Hobbit House patrons had long hair, as does Freddie, who joked from the stage about how many Marcos supporters were probably in the audience. The customers pealed with in-crowd glee and demanded more verses of Freddie's protest tunes. They actually sang along. The decor, even the menu, was right out of Greenwich Village or Old Town or North Beach circa 1963. Except that, as always in the Philippines, there was one nightmarish detail: All of the waiters and waitresses were dwarfs. They were tugging at my blazer hem to show me a table, slipping through the crowd at crotch level, delivering orders and scooping up tips with just their little heads visible above the tabletop. A dozen drinks couldn't put this right.

The next day I attended a protest Mass at Baclaran church. There were more people inside than could possibly be in there, people pressed into a single thing, like coral. Americans would have been fainting and breaking into fistfights and having cardiac arrests. But the Aquino supporters beamed and waved the L sign. They were wearing yellow (as in "Tie a Yellow Ribbon Round the Old Oak Tree") in memory of Benigno Aquino, Cory's gunned-down husband. When Cory herself arrived, a visible charge went through the crowd, like a concerned-citizens version of the wave. "COR-EEE! COR-EEE! COR-EEE!" they hollered, but not in a Beatlemania way. They were there to help her. They were there to protect her. They were there to make the world what the world should be.

The homily was spoken by Cardinal Jaime Sin, whose bizarre name led to such local-newspaper headlines as SIN REQUIRES SOBRIETY. He asked business owners to be understanding if employees had to take time off for the upcoming civil disobedience.

Then Cory came to the pulpit to speak, and part of the crowd —the foreign-journalist part—turned ugly, shoving, kicking, and elbowing for position. I was sandwiched against the pulpit's five-foot-high base, my chin practically on the toes of Cory's yellow pumps. I was unable to avoid looking up her dress. She's a direct woman, slightly schoolmarmish, no nonsense about her. Her charisma seems to proceed from her very lack of charismatic qualities —an ordinary citizen made noble by the force of events. It's as if Harry Truman had been murdered by Thomas E. Dewey and Bess was carrying on. Nice legs, incidentally.

The crowd began singing "Bayan Ko" ("My Country"), the anthem of the campaign, written in the 1930s, during American rule. They sang in the clear, harmonious voice that seems to be given to all the world's put-upon people. The words, in Tagalog, mean:

> *My country was seized and driven to misery.*
> *Birds were given the freedom of flight.*
> *Cage them and they will cry*
> *Just like a beautiful country*
> *That has no freedom. . . .*
> *Philippines that I adore,*

Nest of tears and suffering,
My ambition is to see you free.
If our people will unite,
Then this will come to be.

Standing there by the altar with the rest of the press corps, looking out at these nice, determined faces, feeling this appetite for hope, I began to cry. I was standing there like a big fool with tears running down my face. I remember it all from twenty years ago when I was in a crowd like this—the meetings, the marches, the joy of moral certitude, romance amidst the tear gas. I remember the wonderful fight against prejudice, poverty, injustice, a new day dawning. . . . And I remember how it all slipped away and came to shit.

THOSE INSCRUTABLE ORIENTALS

But maybe I should have spared myself the Kleenex. Or maybe not. I don't know. It's simple enough that Marcos was an oinker and overdue to get sugar-cured and hung in the smokehouse. But a lot of other things about the Philippines weren't so simple.

Where were the guerrillas, the New People's Army, the question mark in Aquino's future, while all this was going on? Having Winter Carnival? Nobody seemed to know. I talked to Oswaldo Carbonell, Manila chairman of Bayan, the left-wing umbrella group with close ties to the NPA. Bayan and the NPA had urged a boycott of the election, but no one boycotted it. Now Oswaldo was leading a not very sizable demonstration by student radicals. "We welcome the NPA," he told me in one breath. "The Cory people are with us," he told me in another.

And while the communists were doing nothing, Marcos was doing too much.

Why did the old slyboots invite a Congressional observer

team, an international observer team, and two battalions of newsmen to an election that was supposed to give him legitimacy and then cheat like a professional-wrestling villain? There he was: bent over, pants around his ankles, with his ass pressed against the window of public opinion.

And Marcos left behind a sizable body of crooks and collaborators armed to the teeth, with plenty of money. One thing the deposed president couldn't cram into the American transport planes was all the cats he'd fattened. Will the super-*tutas* sell their polo ponies to buy house trailers for the folks in Smoky Mountain? Will the thugs march off merrily to reeducation camps singing lewd parodies of "Bayan Ko"?

Then there's the economy. As far as I can figure, there's no one anywhere who knows anything about fixing a third-world economy. The last three underdeveloped nations to become relatively prosperous were Taiwan, South Korea, and Singapore, and they all did it under hard-assed dictators like . . . well, sort of like Marcos.

Time for the Santo Niño. It's a small charm that's popular among the Philippine poor, a brass Baby Jesus with a hard-on. You wear it around your neck, and if you're in physical danger, you're supposed to put it in your mouth.

By Saturday, February 15, eight days after the election, protest enthusiasm seemed to have ebbed. Cory Aquino hadn't been seen in public for two days. That night the Philippine National Assembly declared Marcos the winner. I rushed down to the palace for the riots, but there were none, just Bongbong and a BMW full of "junior cronies" driving none too steadily out the palace gate after the private victory party. In the backseat, the son of the Philippine ambassador to the Court of St. James's was so blasted he was falling out of the car window.

An Aquino rally had been called for the next day. Cory supporters were to march to Rizal Park, in the center of Manila. I went out to one of the staging points in Quezon City, a middle-class suburb that is perhaps the most fervently anti-Marcos place in town. Only several hundred protesters were there at the appointed hour, milling around rather pointlessly. Eventually the crowd grew to about a thousand. The caskets of two murdered Aquino supporters were driven by, signaling the start of the march. (Carrying martyrs all over the place in their caskets is a big thing in the Philippines—sort of waving the bloody shirt and what's in it too.)

The marchers, chanting in a desultory way, began to move toward downtown Manila. By the time they'd gone a kilometer, the crowd had quintupled. In another kilometer, it had quintupled again. Only once, at the University of Santo Tomas, did I see a group join the march in an organized way. People just materialized. And all along the six-kilometer route, cheering crowds were hanging banners, flags, selves out of windows and throwing yellow confetti that they'd made by tearing up the Manila Yellow Pages.

By the time we reached Rizal Park—and it wasn't long because the marchers moved at a jog-trot—there were a half million people gathered around a ramshackle portable stage.

The crowd was squeezed even thicker than it had been at Baclaran church. I was with Tony and Betsy West from ABC. When people saw we were reporters, they somehow made way, moved where there was no room to move. "Foreign press!" they yelled. "Make way! Foreign press!" We were handed through the mob, right to second row front on the center aisle.

The crowd chanted, "COR-EEE! COR-EEE!" in a fearful thunderous rumble that made your lungs and liver swing like bell clappers in the rib cage. Then they began to sing. To hear half a million people sing "Bayan Ko" is . . . is like hearing half a million people sing anything. Even the theme song to *The Jetsons* would have been stirring.

Cory Aquino stepped to the microphones. The crowd was in the kind of frenzy, passion, rapture, transport, wild excitement, or enthusiasm that sends a man to the thesaurus.

But did Cory give a rousing speech, calling for the head of Ferdinand Marcos and telling her countrymen, "Cry havoc, and let slip the dogs of war"?

She did no such thing. In her calm, high-pitched voice and

best head-librarian manner she outlined a program of tame dissent. There'd be a national day of prayer, when people should take off work and go to church, she said. She asked the audience to boycott seven banks and certain other "crony corporations," including the San Miguel brewery. She asked them to delay paying their electric and water bills. And she requested a "noise barrage"—a traditional Philippine protest—each evening after she'd spoken to them over a church-owned AM station. "And you should experiment with other forms of nonviolent protest yourselves," she said, "and let us know how they work."

That was it. Keep your money in a sock. Don't drink beer. And bang garbage-can lids together when you listen to the radio. Betsy, Tony, and I walked away scratching our heads. The crowd dispersed quietly.

Ten days later, they had the country.

Just One of Those Days

~~~~~~

The alarm went off about half an hour late, and I pulled out the old Smith & Wesson 9mm automatic I keep under my pillow and squeezed off a couple of rounds at the fucker. I didn't even have my eyes open yet but I still managed to nick the snooze button. *Kee-rist*, I hate to get up in the morning, but I swear they're going to kill me if I'm late to work again. They killed a couple of other executives just last week—hauled them into the freight elevator and shot them in the head. But I would have gone back to sleep anyway—really—if it hadn't been for this old bitch in the apartment next door. She was putting her cat out for keeps. She must have taken six shots at the thing and the sucker just wouldn't die. It was howling bloody murder. I threw a couple of slugs through the wall in her general direction and then hit the deck and belly-crawled to the kitchen while she returned fire. Using the dishwasher for cover, I made myself a cup of coffee and then I slipped out onto the fire escape and popped a white phosphorus grenade through the old bat's window so I could shower and shave standing up.

Then I couldn't find any clean shirts. And when I did find one it took me twenty minutes to disarm the plastique charge the fucking Chinaman had pressed behind the shirt cardboard. I finally had to set it off in the sink. It was a brand-new shirt too. And the explosion about wrecked the kitchen. The apartment was a mess anyway. Good thing the cleaning lady was coming and a double good thing I had the cleaning lady's kid tied up and booby-trapped in the hall closet or she'd never do windows.

So I was all dressed and ready to go to work, but my date was still asleep, lying on her back with her mouth open, snoring. Even with all the sirens and the fire trucks and the commotion next door, she hadn't stirred. I don't know, somehow this really pissed me off, so I picked her up and threw her through the window. My place is only on the third floor so she probably lived. I'll call her next week and apologize.

The mail hadn't come yet either. The doorman said there was a company of Marines trying to get through with it, but they were pinned down in Murray Hill somewhere. The doorman was as surly as usual and would have slit my throat if I hadn't judo-flipped him and kicked him in the solar plexus first.

I was going to drive to work but then I remembered the parking garage up by the office was still under siege. A dozen spook parking attendants were in there holding about thirty school kids from the suburbs. The kids had come in town for the circus. I don't know why they bothered. Some Puerto Rican meat hunters had got all the elephants already. Anyway, I couldn't get in to park even though I've got a monthly slot. Besides, day before yesterday, the spooks put some of the school kids in this one Cadillac, set it on fire, and drove it off the garage roof. I guess about ten pedestrians were killed when it landed.

Now, I had my favorite little personal-defense unit out of my briefcase and ready as soon as I hit the street. This is a Walther MPK 9mm submachine gun I had special-ordered with selective fire. It doesn't pack quite the punch that an Uzi does, but it's the most compact automatic-fire weapon made in the world, at least in 9mm. I'm a real bug on 9mm ammo. It's kind of my hobby.

By this time, the morning rush hour was in full swing and I couldn't even get a cab in my peep sights, so I had to take the subway. I hate taking the subway—all those kids that spray graffiti all over the place. The cops ought to tie them up and cut their noses off, which is exactly what the cops are doing except they don't catch enough of them for my money. Plus it was a regular shitty morning outside, raining and cold, and bombs were dropping in the next block. And I bet twenty snipers took a shot at me between my building and the subway station. I don't know why those people are allowed out on the streets—they can't hit a goddam thing. Although one did get a bag lady right by the newsstand and got brains all over my raincoat, which I had just got back from the cleaner's. And that wasn't easy either. In fact, it took a midnight raid on the manager's house in Rego Park, where I picked off all four of his guard dogs with the help of a starlight scope. So there I was with brains all over me and then I had to beat the shit out of the blind guy at the newsstand before he'd give me a paper.

I shot my way past a couple of transit cops at the token booth, jumped the turnstile, and got a train to stop by pushing some lady out on the tracks. It's surprising, even a hundred-pound woman can derail those babies when they're going at full throttle, so they generally try to stop if they can. On the train a pack of asshole teenagers was terrorizing everybody, ripping gold chains off women and taking wallets at knifepoint, so I joined them for a while and picked up a little, you know, cab fare. Then I forced everybody, including the conductor, to get in the last car, and I pulled the pin and left them back in the tunnel. Sometimes that's the only way you can get a seat. Almost got my butt kicked for that, though— who would have thought one of those kids would be carrying a wire-guided antitank missile? Good thing it bounced off a signal light and ricocheted right back at the kid with the launcher or I would have been hurting. I mean it.

I was late for work for sure by now. The subway was running way behind schedule, and I had to help the engineer for a while when we ran across an armored train. It must have been from over on the IND line. Anyway, it was shooting up the 34th Street station. Fortunately I'd planted some radio-detonated Claymore mines under the litter baskets in that station just a week back. And I had the transmitter in my briefcase. It's great; it doubles as a digital travel clock. The mines killed all the people on the platform and brought a big section of the tunnel roof down on those guys from the IND too.

Well, by the time I blasted my way through the reception area and raped my secretary and piled up the desk and some chairs to barricade myself in my office, the "old man" was really fuming. He was over on the roof of the building across the street with about twenty guys from accounting, and all of them had M-16s and tear-gas-grenade launchers. He was giving me a real talking-to over the bullhorn, telling me to come out with my hands up or forget about that raise. I got my gas mask on and pulled the Browning automatic rifle out from behind the file cabinet and gave him a little argument. But I couldn't keep that up for long. I had to take some calls and dictate a bunch of letters and it was a real pain in the ass giving dictation to a secretary who was coughing and gagging from the CS gas and threatening a sexual-harassment suit.

Then I had the Peterson contract to straighten out. They manufacture designer jeans, and what a bunch of hard-nosed sons of bitches they are. Their CEO had been on the horn to me all week threatening to nuke our Tarrytown office if he didn't see some action soon. Here was a client who was definitely hanging by a thread. And I knew if that Peterson thing fell through my ass would be in deep shit.

I didn't have time to go out for lunch, so I just had a deli owner and his family killed and some sandwiches sent up. I was working like a bear and by 3:00 I was pretty sure I had all my ducks in a row, and then wouldn't you know it—fifteen megatons right in the parking lot of our suburban branch office. You probably read about it in the papers. It broke half the windows in Manhattan, and I'll bet it takes weeks to decontaminate all the radioactive fallout shit all over the place. And that wasn't the worst of it by any means. Right after Tarrytown goes up in a mushroom cloud and the Peterson account goes with it, the boss finally breaks through my office wall with a Bangalor torpedo and tells me he's promoted young Donovan over my head to group vice-president. That means I'll have to go all the way out to Donovan's house in Darien and poison his kids. Well, that did it. I decided to toss a Molotov cocktail into the mailroom and knock off early.

A couple of the guys and I took our secretaries down to Clark's for a few drinks, raped the girls again, and then gut-shot one of the waiters and bet on how long it would take him to die. I guess I had a few more than I meant to because I was really bushed. So I thought I'd just have a burger in the back room. I wanted to carve it right out of the cow myself but the fucker wouldn't hold still. Finally I had to hit it with a tranq gun. Then the guys and I tried to take some det cord and wrap it around the cow's ass and make chopped steak like that. But the det cord gave the whole thing a really rotten taste. After that I just said fuck dinner and had a couple more drinks and decided to go back to my place and spend a peaceful night at home for a change.

It was still raining outside and I had to call in an air strike to get a taxi. One of the A-1E Skyraiders finally spotted a Checker on Park Avenue and strafed the hack until he chased it over to me. I held the MPK on the driver all the way back to my place and shot up his gas tank for a tip. Then the doorman tried to kill me again and I had to toss a fragmentation grenade at this lady in the lobby to keep her dog from jumping up on me. So I ended up outside waiting around in the rain while one of the building porters cleaned her guts off the elevator door, and *then* what the fuck do you think I saw? A goddam parking ticket on my car! Jesus, I was pissed. I mean I'm *sure* it was one of those Jewish holidays when the alternate-side-of-the-street parking regulations are supposed to be sus-pended. I mean I'm pretty sure all the Jews aren't killed yet. I would have complained to a cop if he hadn't shot first. And then when I finally did get inside, fucking Carson was on vacation again and that asshole Letterman was hosting *The Tonight Show.* Man, it was just one of those days.

Man and Transportation

Ferrari Refutes the Decline of the West

~~~~~~

We made it from Atlanta to Dallas in twelve and a half hours. But that was because we were just cruising, you know, taking in the scenery and enjoying the local color. Besides, we got stuck in bumper-to-bumper camper traffic all the way to Birmingham. Some big collegiate sports event was under way—the University of South Carolina versus Alabama's Crimson Tide in a varsity dogfight, to judge by the fans. No, no, I won't make fun of those good old boys in their Winnebagos driving since dawn with their good old families all the way from Columbia and Charleston and Beaufort just to root for the team of their choice. No, I won't crack wise about the denizens of that fair corner of the free world, because I feel too good about western civilization. And the reason I feel too good about western civilization is that there I was a living, breathing part of it, in the best damn car I've ever driven, smack in the middle of the best damn country there's ever been on earth. And, also, because cutting in and out of those giant travel homes at a hundred miles an hour is more fun than a Marseilles shore leave, and hardly anybody riding in them threw beer cans at us either. Zoom, zoom, zip, zip, I couldn't have been happier if I'd had a sack full of Iranian radicals to drag behind me.

And they love cars down there. *Love* 'em. The men look, and the women look too. And they smile with honest pleasure just to see something that dangerous-looking doing something that dangerous. But best of all the looks we got were the looks we got from the ten-year-old boys. They'd be back there with their little faces pressed against the glass in the RV back windows, and they'd see this red rocket sled coming up behind them in the $50 lane. It couldn't help but touch your heart, how their eyes lit up and their mouths dropped down, as if Santa'd brought them an entire real railroad train. You could all but hear the pitter-patter of the sneakers on their feet as they ran up front and started jerking on their dads' Banlon shirt collars, jumping up and down and yelling and pointing out the windshield, *"Didja see it?! Didja see it, Dad?! Didja?! Didja?! Didja?! Didja?!"*

We came by a 930 Turbo Porsche near the Talladega exit. He was going about ninety when we passed him, and he gave us a little bit of a run, passed us at about 110, and then we passed him again. He was as game as anybody we came across and was hanging right on our tail at 120. Ah, but then—then we just *walked* away from him. Five seconds and he was nothing but a bathtub-shaped dot in the mirrors. I suppose he could have kept up, but driving one of those ass-engined Nazi slot cars must be a task at around 225 percent of the speed limit. But not for us. I've got more vibration here on my electric typewriter than we had blasting into Birmingham that beautiful morning in that beautiful car on a beautiful tour across this wonderful country from the towers of Manhattan to the bluffs of Topanga Canyon so fast we filled the appointment logs of optometrists' offices in thirty cities just from people getting their eyes checked for seeing streaks because they'd watched us go by.

P. J. O'Rourke

Don't get me wrong; we weren't racing. This was strictly a pleasure drive. We had a leisurely lunch in Tuscaloosa, had long talks with every gas-station attendant we saw (and at about nine miles a gallon with a nineteen-gallon tank, we saw them all), and ran into some heavy rain in Louisiana too—had to slow down to practically a hundred, as it was a two-lane road. And then in Shreveport we had a big steak dinner with lots of cocktails and coffee and dessert and Rémy Martin. Why, really, we just *strolled* into Dallas on that third day of a week during which I had more fun than I have ever had doing anything that didn't involve young women. And this kind of fun lasted longer. And I never fell asleep on top of it.

Actually, the trip didn't start out all that well. The idea was . . . well, I'm not quite sure what the idea was. But Ferrari North America, which is based in Montvale, New Jersey, had a 308GTS that needed to be delivered to Los Angeles by January 2, to be featured in a movie. Ferrari called *Car and Driver* and asked if they'd like to assign someone to drive it across the country. *Car and Driver* was good enough to ask me, and of course I said yes. But I had misgivings. Like anyone who loves cars, I'd been fantasizing about Ferraris since before I knew how to say the name. *Fur-rare-ies,* I thought they were. But in my imagination they still all looked like Testa Rossas. In recent years they'd gotten a bit beyond me; I didn't know what to make of these modern pasta-bender luxo-boxes with price tags in the early ionosphere. They have their engines in sideways and backwards, and you sit down on the floor where you can't see your fenders, your feet, or the road. Or that's the way they seemed to me when I sat in one at the auto show, which was the only time I ever had sat in one. And because they were so funny-looking, I assumed they were hard to drive. Besides, I'm opposed on principle to things with wheels that cost more than $20,000 (and don't have "Atchison, Topeka, and Santa Fe" written down the side). Why, there are people starving in Italy. Or going hungry, anyway. Well, maybe not hungry, but I'll bet they don't have enough closet space and the kids have to share a bed-

103

room. And I had some other problems too. I have a daytime job where I'm editor of the *National Lampoon* and I had fallen grievously behind in potty jokes, racial slurs, and comments that demean women. Deadlines loomed, the art department was in a pet, and down at the printing plant they were snarling in their cages. I had no business taking off just then to go do something silly in a rolling red expense account. So I wasn't as enthusiastic about this project as I might have been, especially when I had to go tell my boss, the president of the *National Lampoon's* parent corporation, that I had chosen this extremely inconvenient week to go on a cross-country screw-around for the benefit of another magazine. Now this boss of mine, Julian Weber, is a cold, taciturn, hard-eyed Harvard Law School graduate, about fifty years old, always dressed in a suit, and a very square sort of fellow. And as I was standing in front of his desk, backing and filling and making up lies, he began to frown with great concentration. What I was saying was, "I know it doesn't seem like I've been here very much lately but I've . . . uh . . . been working at home a lot," but what I was thinking was where I could get the boxes I would need when I cleaned out my desk.

Then he blurted it out: "Can I go too?"

The next thing I knew, I was sitting in the parking lot at Ferrari, sitting way down on the floor of this $45,000 atomic doorstop, completely puzzled by the controls; and sitting rather stiffly in the bucket seat next to me was my goddam boss. At least he had a pair of blue jeans on, but his blue jeans had been *pressed,* with a perfect crease across each knee. I don't know if they sell blue jeans at Brooks Brothers, but if they do that's where he'd bought these. I couldn't figure out what it was going to be like, cooped up for a week in a car with somebody and unable to discuss drugs or teenaged girls. I also couldn't figure out how to work the car. Everyone at Ferrari was on Christmas vacation; the keys had been left with the receptionist. There wasn't even anyone there to look properly worried, let alone to show me how to start the thing. And the Ferrari manual was translated from Italian to English by someone who spoke only Chinese. "Well," said Mr. Weber, "I'm ready to go now."

I remembered that Bill Baker, Ferrari's director of public relations, had told me, "Be sure not to ———— or you'll foul the plugs." But what it was that I wasn't supposed to ————, I had no idea. So, finally, I just started it up and very tentatively, very nervously drove it out onto the Garden State Parkway, where the plugs immediately fouled. We coasted onto the berm. I got the car started again and out into traffic and it loaded up and stalled. I got it started another time and it began to misfire and choke, and I had to stick it in third and run it up over five grand just to keep the engine moving.

"I thought you knew how to drive one of these," said my boss. And I had to keep it in third all the way to Trenton before the plugs cleared. A solid wall of dirty traffic was pressing in from every side while I sat perspiring, not a fender in sight, waiting for some passing jackass in a Peterbilt to make a belly tank out of us. I got off the turnpike at Wilmington and headed down the Delmarva Peninsula. The car seemed to be running all right, but now Julian wanted to drive. I was afraid that if he didn't keep the revs up, we'd stall again, and I couldn't explain to him how to drive the car because I hadn't the slightest idea myself, and, besides, I just didn't feel like riding along at fifty-five with this lawyer type at the wheel telling me how foreign cars of this kind seemed "quite unusual in their method of operation" or some such. I mean, Julian's a New Yorker, and New Yorkers think all cars are yellow and have lights on the roof. So I held him off down past Dover, but he was beginning to insist, and he's my boss, and what could I do?

We had just turned off onto Route 1 along Delaware Bay when I put him behind the wheel. Route 1 is a brand-new road, four lanes wide and butter-smooth, built to carry hordes of picnic-prone Wilmingtonians down to the ocean shore. But in December there's nothing and nobody in sight. Julian settled into the driver's seat and gave the *Millennium Falcon*–like controls a momentary glance. Then he stamped on the accelerator with an expensive loafer and redlined the 308 up through the gears to a hundred miles an hour through the potato fields and abandoned burger stands without time to even take his hand off the shift lever until he hit fifth, and when he did have time to take his hand off he used that hand to plop a Blondie cassette into the Blaupunkt and a quarter-ton of decibels came on with "Die Young Stay Pretty," and the scenery exploded in the distance, bush and tree debris flying at us while my eyeballs pressed all the way back into the medulla, and that quadruple-throated three-quart V-8 wound up beyond the vocal range of Maria Callas, *Eeeeeeeeeeeeeeeeeeeeeeeeeeeeeeeeeeeeeeeeeeeeeee-eeeeeeeeeeeeeeeeeeeeeeeeeeeeee*, leaving, I'm sure, a trail of shattered stemware in the more prosperous of the farmhouses we passed along our way.

And so it was Julian, my sobersided superior in the corporate hierarchy, who turned out to be the real leadfoot. He spent his half of the driving time doing a very credible imitation of Wolfgang von Trips, while I spent my half of the driving time nervously looking for cops. He turned out to be a pretty good guy, too, for a lawyer. (Although, to protect his marriage and business career, his views on drugs and teenaged girls will go unrecorded.) Anyway, it was that moment out on Delaware Route 1 that changed the entire complexion of the trip.

I guess what we were supposed to be doing with the car was to see if it could perform the function for which it was built. That function is high-speed touring, and the answer is YES, carved in those monumental granite letters that once were used for the title frames in movies like *El Cid*. The Ferrari isn't much to bop around town in. It's necessarily stiff and uncompromising at low speeds. And you'd sooner dock a sailboat in a basement utility sink than try to parallel-park it. But turn the son of a bitch loose on the open road and it's as though you've died and gone to hot-rod heaven. True, the 308 wasn't designed, really, for American touring, where the speed limit is fifty-five and distances are measured in thousands of miles instead of hundreds of kilometers. There's nary a gear in the box where the Ferrari will do fifty-five with pleasure, and the luggage space wouldn't make a good ice bucket. But the answer to those complaints is, Who gives a good goddam? You drive this car for an hour, a hundred miles down the coast between the dunes, with the cattails waving in the tidal marshes and the winter surf crashing on the sea walls, through a blur of empty resort towns with the afternoon sun down low and Edward Hopper—bright across the landscape—you do that for an hour and you'll kill for this car. You'll murder people in their beds just to get back behind the wheel.

We slipped down the eastern shore of Maryland, on into that tag end of Virginia below Assateague Island and out onto the Chesapeake Bay Bridge Tunnel. This eighteen-mile ocean transit is nearly as awesome a piece of engineering as what we were driving and a sight of heart-aching beauty in the moonlight. We launched ourselves down the trestle causeway, flying low above the water, then plunging into the sea like a depth charge and up onto the high-level bridges like an epiphany in a *New Yorker* short story. At Norfolk we pitched into the narrow, twisting roads along the North Carolina border and went, just wreathed in shit-eating grins, all the way to Greensboro.

We chose Greensboro for the night because there's a Ferrari dealer there. And the car, joy that it was, was not running right. We kept loosing power, especially when Julian was driving—a seat-of-the-pants problem, as it turned out. Under the 308's driver seat there's a cutoff switch that kills the engine after five seconds without weight on the seat cushion. This is in case you turn turtle and are lying on your head with gasoline running down your leg. The kill switch keeps the car from becoming a Molotov cocktail. Julian is a boss, but he's not a *big* boss, and he just didn't generate enough down-force to keep the switch from unswitching. This thingamabob is an admirable safety device, no doubt, but we had the Greensboro dealer yank it. Then we had him tune up the car and send the bill to Ferrari North America.

Julian and I set out to try for the nighttime fast-driving-and-scotch-drinking-with-a-large-dinner record time to Atlanta. The car was even faster, even smoother than before and absolutely bullet-proof now. We would put nearly three thousand more miles on it, most of them at over a hundred miles an hour, and the solitary mechanical problem we would have between Greensboro and L.A. would be the electric antenna's bezel vibrating itself off somewhere in east Texas, so that when I put the antenna up it shot six feet out of the right rear fender, trailing its line like a harpoon into the middle of the LBJ Hilton parking lot.

It was on our way to Atlanta that Julian and I began to feel really at home in the Ferrari, began to feel sharp with its stiff little clutch and slim shift gates and with the frightening immediacy of its steering—straight from your left brain to the road. We even began to feel comfortable half-recumbent in that mousehole cockpit filled with levers and toggles and with hardly enough room for candy bars and tape cassettes. Maps, flashlights, and sunglasses bulged out of the leather pockets on the doors. The radar detector was clipped on the right sun visor with its controls in the passenger's face and its patch cord to the cigarette lighter tangling his every move. But we felt we could stay in there for a whole Apollo mission if only we had relief tubes.

We screamed along in the night with a tape of Bruce Springsteen's street-racing songs for a score in a car that had ceased to seem strange or exotic or even pretty. Now it just seemed like the apotheosis of perfect speed from perfect function through perfection of design to the perfection of our mood. And there we were in something that could outhandle anything it couldn't outrun, and there wasn't *anything* it couldn't outrun.

When we got to Atlanta, the band in the hotel bar was the worst thing we'd ever heard. But it didn't matter. Nothing could cloud our outlook. Ralph Nader himself would have been welcome at our table, so infected were we with the spirit of superiority to the humdrum concerns of daily life. I mean this car does one thing. It makes you happy.

And the car did one more thing for me. It reaffirmed my belief in America. It may sound strange to say that a $45,000 Italian sports car reaffirmed my belief in America, but, as I said, it's all part of western civilization and here we were in America, the apogee of that fine trend in human affairs. And, after all, what have we been getting civilized *for*, all these centuries? Why did we fight all those wars, conquer all those nations, kidnap all those Africans, and kill all the Indians in the western hemisphere? Why, for *this!* For this perfection of knowledge and craft. For this conquest of the physical elements. For this sense of mastery of man over nature. To be in control of our destinies—and there is no more profound feeling of control over one's destiny that I have ever experienced than to drive a Ferrari down a public road at 130 miles an hour. Only God can make a tree, but only man can drive by one that fast. And if the lowly Italians, the lamest, silliest, least stable of our NATO allies, can build a machine like this, just think what it is that *we* can do. We can smash the atom. We can cure polio. We can fly to the moon if we like. There is nothing we can't do. Maybe we don't happen to build Ferraris, but that's not because there's anything wrong with America. We just haven't turned the full light of our intelligence and ability in that direction. We were, you know, busy elsewhere. We may not have Ferraris but just think what our Polaris-missile submarines are like. And if it feels like this in a Ferrari at 130, my God, what can it possibly feel like at Mach 2.5 in an F-15? Ferrari 308s and F-15s—these are the conveyances of free men. What do the Bolshevik automatons know of destiny and its control? What have we to fear from the barbarous Red hordes?

Actually, at the time when this thought occurred to me we were out in west Texas, half a thousand miles from any population center or major military base, so Julian and I probably had nothing at all to fear from the barbarous Red hordes. The highway patrol, however, was another matter. You may wonder how we kept ourselves from being fined into starvation or, anyway, thrown into jail during this transmigration. The credit for that goes all to the radar detector. After a couple of days we learned to read the machine so that we could tell even at what angle the radar gun was pointed and whether it was in a moving patrol car or a stationary one. In fact, our biggest legal danger lay not in getting apprehended by the police but in apprehending them, coming up over some rise at 110 or 120 and rocketing up the tailpipe of an unsuspecting smokey. We spent a lot of time peering down the road trying to figure out what we were about to overtake, and every time we crossed a state line we had to spend about an hour figuring out what that state's patrol cars looked like. But, as it was, we only got one ticket all week. It was on the last night, right after the New Year's weekend, in jammed-solid, rush-hour-like traffic from Las Vegas to Los Angeles. We were in California, where the highway patrol doesn't even have radar, and all we were trying to do was get around one carload of vacationers to get stuck behind the next when we were pulled over. Officer Huyenga (as best I can make out his signature on the ticket) was politeness itself and should be promoted to governor. "It's a shame," he said, "to have a car like this and only be able to go fifty-five." We suppressed a chuckle, and I believe he did too, and so we got our only ticket—for going ten miles an hour over the limit.

From Atlanta to Dallas we'd stayed on the Interstates, but once past Fort Worth we took the empty, two-laned U.S. 180 across the astonishing west-Texas landscape and then, in the twilight, through the big mesas that make up the southeast corner of New Mexico. There we got into our only other real race of the trip, with a pickup truck full of drunk bauxite miners or some such, and those boys could really drive a pickup truck. They held their own up through a hundred miles an hour on the curves and bends into Carlsbad, and then we left them and went back into Texas down switchbacks and hairpins skirting the edges of Guadalupe Peak. This was where I first discovered why you wear driving gloves. I'd always thought they make you look like a golf pro, but somebody had given me a pair as a going-away present and I found that you wear them because of how much your palms sweat when you're scared. But the Ferrari was just as solid at ninety and a hundred in the mountains as it had been at 130 in the straights. Nothing that either of us ever did so much as made one tire blush with the thought of wavering from its appointed course. In fact, the only thing that made the mountains exciting was that although the Ferrari wasn't going to put us over the side, there was every chance that Julian or I might. But we didn't, and we drove into El Paso for the evening.

No matter how many times you've seen it, it's incredible the way the cities of the Southwest pop up from nowhere at night— vast, glowing fairylands. Although in this particular fairyland we took a wrong turn and wound up with an accidental ten-minute tour of Ciudad Juárez. The Ferrari startled the Mexican customs official into a ballet of Señor-you-may-pass-through-with-pleasure-with-honor-with-gratitude pantomimes. I'm sure it made his night. The Mexican customs official startled us, too, because that was when we discovered we were in Mexico; with horrible visions of Ferrari confiscations, I got turned around and headed back to America. The American customs officials were also extremely courteous. I guess they figured that whatever it was we were smuggling we'd already smuggled it and were happily living off the proceeds, so it was too late now. Juárez, incidentally, greatly testifies to the value of western civilization by exhibiting no sign of it anywhere.

The next day we drove to Las Vegas. Oh, the pure joy of the thing—knowing that out there, down that road, there's a fellow doing sixty-five or seventy, a little nervous, watching for cops, maybe his wife's telling him to slow down, and then screaming out of nowhere comes something not half his height, an eardrum-popping Doppler whizz just beneath the very bone point of his left elbow resting on the window frame. *Whaizzat??!!!* What *was* that??!! We could see his bumper wiggle behind us as he'd give the wheel a startled jerk, and we'd be in the next county before that fellow'd regain his composure.

Julian hit the record high speed of our trip—140, on I-10 going into Deming, New Mexico. And at Lordsburg we turned off onto U.S. 70 up into the mountains and Indian reservations east of Phoenix and from there across the desert all the way to Lake

Mead. And we didn't meet a single dislikable person. Not that day or any other, from the puzzled receptionist at Ferrari North America to Officer Huyenga of the California Highway Patrol. Fine, upstanding, friendly, outgoing Americans who wanted to know how fast it would go, every one. It was truly heartening. The nicest bunch of people you'd ever care to meet. It made me wish I didn't belong to the Republican Party and the NRA just so I could go out and join both to defend it all. And rolling through the desert thus, I worked myself into a great patriotic frenzy, which culminated on the parapets of Hoover Dam (even if that was kind of a socialistic project and built by the Roosevelt in the wheelchair and not by the good one who killed bears). With the Ferrari parked up atop that orgasmic arc of cement, doors flung open and Donna Summer's "Bad Girls" blasting into the night above the rush of a man-crafted Niagara and the crackle and the hum of mighty dynamos, I was uplifted, transported, ecstatic. A black man in a big, solid Eldorado pulled up next to us and got out to shake our hands. "You passed me this morning down in New Mexico," he said. "And that sure is a beautiful car. And you sure must have been moving because I've been going ninety on the turnpike all day and haven't stopped for anything but gas and I just caught up with you now." But we hadn't been on the turnpike, we told him. We'd been all through the mountains and had stopped for lunch and had been caught in Phoenix traffic half the afternoon. "Goddam!" he said. "That's *beautiful!*" Now where on the face of God's green earth are you going to find a country with people like that in it? Answer me that and tell me anyplace but here and I'll strangle you for a communist spy.

That was New Year's Eve, and we celebrated that night in the MGM Grand. I'm sorry to say that the Ferrari does not confer great good fortune at the blackjack table. But we were paid a fine compliment the next day at Caesar's Palace. Instead of making us wait for valet parking, the lot jockey rushed up to us where we were fifth or sixth in line. "No receipt necessary for *you,* sir," he said, and swept the car around in a tight U-turn and parked it right in front.

And that evening we headed up the Barstow incline to Los Angeles and got our ticket and I dropped Julian off so he could return to the staid world of business acumen, if he can. I kept the Ferrari for as long as I could the next day, roving around Beverly Hills and driving up and down Mulholland Drive, but it had to be delivered to Ferrari's West Coast headquarters in Compton by five o'clock. It was a terrible thing to give it back, but I headed down the Harbor Freeway feeling every bit as good as I had for every moment since we first hit a hundred back in Delaware. It was a glow that wouldn't fade. And I still felt good when I flipped the keys onto the receptionist's desk. And I still felt good when I hopped into the limousine I'd thoughtfully charged to *Car and Driver* to ease the pain of transition. And, in fact, I still feel good today.

But the story ends on a sad note. The movie that this incredible car traveled all that way to be in will be called *Don't Eat the Yellow Snow in Hawaii,* so maybe western civilization hasn't quite been perfected yet.

High-Speed
Performance
Characteristics of
Pickup Trucks

~~~~~~

I'm an experienced pickup truck driver. I was driving my pickup the other Saturday night after having—as I made very clear to the police—hardly anything to drink and while going—honest, officer —about thirty miles an hour when, I swear, a deer ran into the road, and I was forced to pull off the highway with such abruptness that it took the wrecker crew six hours to get my truck out of the woods.

An experienced pickup truck driver is a person who's wrecked one. An inexperienced pickup truck driver is a person who's about to wreck one. A *very* inexperienced pickup truck driver doesn't even own a pickup but will probably be mistaken for a wild antelope by people jack-lighting pronghorns in somebody else's pickup truck. The foremost high-speed-handling characteristic of pickup trucks is the remarkably high speed with which they head from wherever you are directly into trouble. This has to do with beer. The minute you get in a pickup you want a beer. I'm not exactly sure why this is, but personally I blame it on Jimmy Carter having been President.

You see, everyone in America has always wanted to be a redneck. That's why all those wig-and-knicker colonial guys moved to Kentucky with Davy Crockett even before he got his TV show. And witness aristocratic young Theodore Roosevelt's attempt to be a "rough rider." Even Henry James used the same last name as his peckerwood cousin Jesse. And as Henry James would tell you, if anyone read him anymore and also if he were still alive, the single most prominent distinguishing feature of the redneck is that he drives a pickup truck. This explains why all of us are muscling these things around downtown Minneapolis and Cincinnati.

You may be wondering where Jimmy Carter comes in. Well, Jimmy Carter was a redneck just like we're all trying to be, but he was a sober redneck. Most of us had never seen a sober redneck, and we have the Reagan landslide to testify that none of us ever want to see one again. It was a horrifying apparition. And ever since Jimmy Carter all of us rednecks have had to be very careful to be *drunk* rednecks lest we turn into some kind of awful creature with big buck teeth and a State Department full of human-rights yahoos.

Thus the pickup truck has become the world's only beer-guided motor vehicle. Let's examine one unit of this guidance system. Let's examine another. Let's examine the whole six-pack. Now let's drive over and see if any ducks have come in on Hodge Pond. Whoops! Crash! Forgot the camper back wasn't bolted down.

THE PICKUP: DESIGN AND ENGINEERING

A pickup truck is basically a back porch with an engine attached. Both a pickup and a back porch are good places to drink beer because you can take a leak standing up from either. Pickup trucks are generally a little faster downhill than back porches, with the exception of certain California back porches during mudslide season. But back porches get better gas mileage.

Another important difference between back porches and pickup trucks is the suspension systems. Back porches are most often seated firmly on the ground by means of cement-block foundations. Nothing nearly that sophisticated is used in pickup trucks. The front suspension of a modern pickup truck is fully independent. Each wheel is independently bolted right to the frame. The rear suspension is a live axle usually attached by a rope to someone else's bumper while he tries to pull you out of the woods.

This suspension design is ideal for use in conjunction with the pickup's 100 percent front/0 percent rear weight distribution. This weight distribution is achieved through engine placement. The engine is placed just where you'd place it on a back porch—hanging off one end so you can get under it and take a look at the giant dent in the oil pan you got when you ran over the patio furniture last night.

Theoretically such forward-weight bias should cause gross understeer. But everyone involved with pickup trucks is whooping it up too much to have any grasp of theory, so the forward-weight bias causes oversteer instead. What happens to an unloaded pickup truck in a curve is that the rear end has nothing to do—is unemployed, metaphorically speaking—so it comes around to ask you for work, up there in the front of the truck where all the weight is. And the result is exactly like one of those revolving restaurants that they have on hotels except it's on four bald snow tires instead of a hotel, and it's in the middle of the highway, and it tips over.

In order to correct this handling problem, the pickup's load bed is filled with leaf mulch, garden loam, hundred-pound bags of dog food, two snowmobiles, half a cord of birch logs, your son's Cub Scout pack, and a used refrigerator to put beer in out on the back porch. The result is an adjusted weight bias of 0 percent front/100 percent rear that causes a handling problem different from either understeer or oversteer, which is no steering at all because the front wheels aren't touching the ground.

The same kind of thinking that went into pickup truck suspension design has also been applied to the pickup engine, which is basically the same device Jim Watt was using to pump water out of coal mines in 1810 except that, in accordance with recent EPA rulings, a hanky soaked in Pinsol has been stuffed into each cylinder to cut down on exhaust emissions. There are three types of pickup truck engines: the six-cylinder engine, which does not have enough cylinders; the eight-cylinder engine, which has too many; and the four-cylinder engine, which is found in "mini pickups" driven by people who think John Denver is the right kind of redneck to be and believe they can talk to whales. The less said about four-cylinder engines the better. But all these engines have a common fault in that they continue to run after the ignition has been switched off, a phenomenon known as "dieseling." Engines that actually *are* diesels have been introduced for pickup trucks and they rectify this problem by not starting in the first place.

It doesn't matter. The real power for pickup trucks is generated inside the gearbox, or at least it seems to be because it's so noisy in there. And if it isn't, it soon will be after you get blotto and start shifting without the clutch.

There are usually five gears in a pickup. One is a mystery gear which is illustrated on the shift knob but cannot be found. Then there is first gear, which is good for getting stuck in the woods. When you aren't stuck in the woods it's good for yanking your bumper off while trying to help a friend who owns a pickup when *he's* stuck in the woods. First gear has a top speed of three. Third gear has a slightly higher top speed but you can't climb a speed bump without downshifting and the truck still only gets eight mpg. It is not known exactly what third gear is for. All normal pickup truck driving is done in second. Pickups also have a reverse gear, which is good for getting more completely stuck in the woods than first gear can do alone.

Because pickup trucks get stuck in the woods so often, four-wheel drive has become a popular option. The four-wheel-drive feature is either operated by a lever which fails to put the truck in 4WD or by a lever which fails to take it out. Four-wheel drive allows you to mire four wheels axle-deep in the woods instead of just two.

Perhaps the most novel aspect to pickup truck engineering is that pickups have no brakes. True, there is a parking brake which, if you set it, allows you to let your driverless pickup roll downhill into a busy intersection with a clear conscience. And there is a brake pedal, but stepping on it only produces a poignant desire for one more beer before you crash into the woods. There are, however, a number of methods of bringing a pickup truck to a stop, most of them involving trees in those woods, but sometimes the spare tire, which hangs down behind the bumper in the back, will fall partly out of its mounting and produce drag force. And very often a pickup will run out of gas and coast to a stop. And right in front of a bar, too—according to what you told your wife.

That just goes to show how thoroughgoing the relationship is between pickups and drinking. I mean it sure looks like these things were designed by people who'd been drinking. And the level of finish indicates they were built by people who'd been drinking. It only stands to reason they should be driven by people like us who are half in the bag. As a result, the most popular pickup truck performance modification is—you guessed it—having a drink. For instance, at sixty miles an hour take a tight turn and notice that if you *hadn't* been tight you never would have taken that turn in the first place. Now you call a wrecker and I'll go get some tall ones.

DRIVING TECHNIQUE

Driving a pickup at high speed is a difficult skill to master. The first step is to assume the proper driving position: Use one hand to firmly grasp the drip rail on the roof. This takes the place of shoulder harness, lap belt, and air bag and lets you give the finger to people with anti-handgun bumper stickers on their cars. Then place your other hand on the gearshift knob so you'll always know what gear you're in (which is second, as I pointed out before). Now take your third hand . . . Perhaps some picture of the difficulty is beginning to emerge. Anyway, be sure to balance your beer can carefully in your lap.

The second step is to drive over to the 7-Eleven and get more beer. Use your down vest to mop up the one you spilled all over your crotch as you backed out the driveway.

The third step is cornering technique. There are three ways to take a high-speed curve in a pickup. The first way is to use the traditional racecar driver's "late apex": Go deep into the curve at full speed doing all your downshifting and useless brake-pedal pumping in a straight line. Then, in one smooth motion, turn the wheel to the full extent necessary for the curve. Aim for an apex slightly past the geometrical apex of the inside edge of the curve and slowly bring the steering wheel back to straight ahead as you reapply the throttle. This will put your truck into the woods. The second way to take a fast curve is to come into the curve slightly slower, dial in a greater amount of steering, and stay on the throttle so as to propel the truck into a "power slide." This will put your truck in the woods too. The third method is to come to a full stop before entering the curve and have a beer. While you're doing that someone else will come along in another pickup truck and knock you into the woods anyway.

Now that you've wrecked a pickup and are an experienced pickup truck driver, it's important to know what to tell the police. Tell them a deer ran into the road. This happens very frequently in the places where we rednecks live, especially when we've been drinking. For example, below are the five most common explanations made to the North Carolina Highway Patrol by drivers who have put their pickup trucks into the woods:

1. A deer ran into the road.
2. A deer ran into the road.

3. A deer ran into the road.

4. A deer ran into the road.

5. I was stopped at a stop sign but I had to start up again real fast and run my pickup into the woods because otherwise it would have been smashed by this deer that ran into the road.

PURCHASE, REPAIR, AND MAINTENANCE OF THE HIGH-PERFORMANCE PICKUP TRUCK

If, however, you still haven't wrecked a pickup truck and are weighing the obvious delights of having an opportunity to do so against such considerations as wanting to be a redneck but only having enough money to be middle-class or having a wife who thought she was marrying a college-educated account executive, here are some points for you to consider. First, how much will a pickup truck cost?

Pickup	$ 9360.00
Beer	2.89
Another pickup to replace first one that you wreck	9360.00
Rabbit for wife, who won't drive truck	8750.00
TOTAL	$27,472.89

That's a fair piece of change. But on the other hand, pickup trucks are virtually maintenance-free. In fact, all pickup repairs can be done with a long chain. Attach one end of the chain to the pickup truck, drop the other end of the chain on the ground, and go buy a real car.

You may also want to know if a pickup truck is truly useful. I'm afraid the answer is yes—all too much so.

P. J. O'Rourke

UTILITY COMPARISON

Pickup vs. Real Car

USE	PICK-UP	REAL CAR
Brush hauling	Yes, I'll do it tomorrow.	Good excuse not to haul brush.
Taking trash to dump	Really, I'll do it tomorrow. The Falcons are playing Dallas.	Call Goodwill.
Furniture loads	Room for five-piece bedroom set and expensive oriental rug.	Have plenty of furniture already, don't need any more.

But, when all is said and done, it really would have looked silly at the end of *Easy Rider* if Peter Fonda and Dennis Hooper had been shot by a couple of guys in a Fiat Brava. And what's life for if you never get a chance to shoot the likes of Peter Fonda and Dennis Hopper? Besides, you'll never really appreciate the profound and astonishing beauties of nature if you don't get stuck in the woods now and then. And you won't appreciate them half as much if you don't have a lot of beer along.

A Cool and Logical Analysis of the Bicycle Menace

And an examination of the actions necessary to license, regulate, or abolish entirely this dreadful peril on our roads

〜〜〜〜〜〜〜〜〜〜〜〜〜〜〜〜〜〜〜〜〜〜〜〜〜〜〜〜〜〜〜〜

Our nation is afflicted with a plague of bicycles. Everywhere the public right-of-way is glutted with whirring, unbalanced contraptions of rubber, wire, and cheap steel pipe. Riders of these flimsy appliances pay no heed to stop signs or red lights. They dart from between parked cars, dash along double yellow lines, and whiz through crosswalks right over the toes of law-abiding citizens like me.

In the cities, every lamppost, tree, and street sign is disfigured by a bicycle slathered in chains and locks. And elevators must be shared with the cycling faddist so attached to his "moron's bathchair" that he has to take it with him everywhere he goes.

In the country, one cannot drive around a curve or over the

crest of a hill without encountering a gaggle of huffing bicyclers spread across the road in suicidal phalanx.

Even the wilderness is not safe from infestation, as there is now such a thing as an off-road bicycle and a horrible sport called "bicycle-cross."

The ungainly geometry and primitive mechanicals of the bicycle are an offense to the eye. The grimy and perspiring riders of the bicycle are an offense to the nose. And the very existence of the bicycle is an offense to reason and wisdom.

PRINCIPAL ARGUMENTS WHICH MAY BE MARSHALED AGAINST BICYCLES

1. BICYCLES ARE CHILDISH.

Bicycles have their proper place, and that place is under small boys delivering evening papers. Insofar as children are too short to see over the dashboards of cars and too small to keep motorcycles upright at intersections, bicycles are suitable vehicles for them. But what are we to make of an adult in a suit and tie pedaling his way to work? Are we to assume he still delivers newspapers for a living? If not, do we want a doctor, lawyer, or business executive who plays with toys? St. Paul, in his First Epistle to the Corinthians, 13:11, said, "When I became a man, I put away childish things." He did *not* say, "When I became a man, I put away childish things and got more elaborate and expensive childish things from France and Japan."

Considering the image projected, bicycling commuters might as well propel themselves to the office with one knee in a red Radio Flyer wagon.

2. BICYCLES ARE UNDIGNIFIED.

A certain childishness is, no doubt, excusable. But going about in public with one's head between one's knees and one's rump protruding in the air is nobody's idea of acceptable behavior.

It is impossible for an adult to sit on a bicycle without looking the fool. There is a type of woman, in particular, who should never assume the bicycling posture. This is the woman of ample proportions. Standing on her own feet she is a figure to admire—classical in her beauty and a symbol, throughout history, of sensuality, maternal virtue, and plenty. Mounted on a bicycle, she is a laughingstock.

In a world where loss of human dignity is such a grave and all-pervading issue, what can we say about people who voluntarily relinquish all of theirs and go around looking at best like Quixote on Rosinante and more often like something in the Macy's Thanksgiving Day parade? Can such people be trusted? Is a person with so little self-respect likely to have any respect for you?

3. BICYCLES ARE UNSAFE.

Bicycles are topheavy, have poor brakes, and provide no protection to their riders. Bicycles are also made up of many hard and sharp components which, in collision, can do grave damage to people and the paint finish on automobiles. Bicycles are dangerous things.

Of course, there's nothing wrong, *per se*, with dangerous things. Speedboats, racecars, fine shotguns, whiskey, and love are all very dangerous. Bicycles, however, are dangerous without being any fun. You can't shoot pheasants with a bicycle or water-ski behind it or go 150 miles an hour or even mix it with soda and ice. And the idea of getting romantic on top of a bicycle is alarming. All you can do with one of these ten-speed sink traps is grow tired and sore and fall off it.

Being dangerous without being fun puts bicycles in a category with open-heart surgery, the war in Vietnam, the South Bronx, and divorce. Sensible people do all that they can to avoid such things as these.

4. BICYCLES ARE UN-AMERICAN.

We are a nation that worships speed and power. And for good reason. Without power we would still be part of England and everybody would be out of work. And if it weren't for speed, it would take us all months to fly to L.A., get involved in the movie business, and become rich and famous.

Bicycles are too slow and impuissant for a country like ours. They belong in Czechoslovakia.

5. I DON'T LIKE THE KIND OF PEOPLE WHO RIDE BICYCLES.

At least I think I don't. I don't actually know anyone who rides a bicycle. But the people I see on bicycles look like organic-gardening zealots who advocate federal regulation of bedtime and want American foreign policy to be dictated by UNICEF. These people should be confined.

I apologize if I have the wrong impression. It may be that bicycle riders are all members of the New York Stock Exchange, Methodist bishops, retired Marine Corps drill instructors, and other solid citizens. However, the fact that they cycle around in broad daylight making themselves look like idiots indicates that they're crazy anyway and should be confined just the same.

6. BICYCLES ARE UNFAIR.

Bicycles use the same roads as cars and trucks yet they pay no gasoline tax, carry no license plates, are not required to have insurance, and are not subject to DOT, CAFE, or NHTSA regulations. Furthermore, bicyclists do not have to take driver's examinations, have eye tests when they're over sixty-five, carry registration papers with them, or submit to breathalyzer tests under the threat of law. And they never get caught in radar traps.

The fact (see No. 5, above) that bicycles are ridden by the very people who most favor government interference in life makes the bicycle's special status not only unfair but an outright incitement to riot.

Equality before the law is the cornerstone of democracy. Bicycles should be made to carry twenty-gallon tanks of gasoline. They should be equipped with twelve-volt batteries and a full complement of taillights, headlamps, and turn signals. They should have seat belts, air bags, and safety-glass windows too. And every bicycle rider should be inspected once a year for hazardous defects and be made to wear a number plate hanging around his neck and another on the seat of his pants.

7. BICYCLES ARE GOOD EXERCISE.

And so is swinging through trees on your tail. Mankind has invested more than four million years of evolution in the attempt to avoid physical exertion. Now a group of backward-thinking atavists mounted on foot-powered pairs of Hula-Hoops would have us pumping our legs, gritting our teeth, and searing our lungs as though we were being chased across the Pleistocene savanna by saber-toothed tigers. Think of the hopes, the dreams, the effort, the brilliance, the pure force of will that, over the eons, has gone into the creation of the Cadillac Coupe de Ville. Bicycle riders would have us throw all this on the ash heap of history.

WHAT MUST BE DONE ABOUT THE BICYCLE THREAT?

Fortunately, nothing. Frustrated truck drivers and irate cabbies make a point of running bicycles off the road. Terrified old ladies jam umbrella ferrules into wheel spokes as bicycles rush by them

P. J. O'Rourke

on sidewalks. And all of us have occasion to back over bicycles that are haplessly parked.

Bicycles are quiet and slight, difficult for normal motorized humans to see and hear. People pull out in front of bicycles, open car doors in their path, and drive through intersections filled with the things. The insubstantial bicycle and its unshielded rider are defenseless against these actions. It's a simple matter of natural selection. The bicycle will be extinct within the decade. And what a relief that will be.

How to Drive Fast
on Drugs While
Getting Your
Wing-Wang
Squeezed and Not
Spill Your Drink

When it comes to taking chances, some people like to play poker or shoot dice; other people prefer to parachute-jump, go rhino hunting, or climb ice floes, while still others engage in crime or marriage. But I like to get drunk and drive like a fool. Name me, if you can, a better feeling than the one you get when you're half a bottle of Chivas in the bag with a gram of coke up your nose and a teenage lovely pulling off her tube top in the next seat over while you're going a hundred miles an hour down a suburban side street. You'd have to watch the entire Mexican air force crash-land in a liquid petroleum gas storage facility to match this kind of thrill. If you ever have much more fun than that, you'll die of pure sensory overload, I'm here to tell you.

But wait. Let's pause and analyze *why* this particular matrix of activities is perceived as so highly enjoyable. I mean, aside from

~~~~~~

the teenage lovely pulling off her tube top in the next seat over. Ignoring that for a moment, let's look at the psychological factors conducive to placing positive emotional values on the sensory end product of experientially produced excitation of the central nervous system and smacking into a lamppost. Is that any way to have fun? How would your mother feel if she knew you were doing this? She'd cry. She really would. And that's how you know it's fun. Anything that makes your mother cry is fun. Sigmund Freud wrote all about this. It's a well-known fact.

Of course, it's a shame to waste young lives behaving this way —speeding around all tanked up with your feet hooked in the steering wheel while your date crawls around on the floor mats opening zippers with her teeth and pounding on the accelerator with an empty liquor bottle. But it wouldn't be taking a chance if you weren't risking *something*. And even if it is a shame to waste young lives behaving this way, it is definitely cooler than risking *old* lives behaving this way. I mean, so what if some fifty-eight-year-old butt-head gets a load on and starts playing Death Race 2000 in the rush-hour traffic jam? What kind of chance is he taking? He's just waiting around to see what kind of cancer he gets anyway. But if young, talented *you*, with all of life's possibilities at your fingertips, you and the future Cheryl Tiegs there, so fresh, so beautiful—if the two of *you* stake your handsome heads on a single roll of the dice in life's game of stop-the-semi—now *that's* taking chances! Which is why old people rarely risk their lives. It's not because they're chicken—they just have too much dignity to play for small stakes.

Now a lot of people say to me, "Hey, P.J., you like to drive fast. Why not join a responsible organization, such as the Sports Car Club of America, and enjoy participation in sports car racing? That way you could drive as fast as you wish while still engaging in a well-regulated spectator sport that is becoming more popular each year." No thanks. In the first place, if you ask me, those guys are a bunch of tweedy old barf mats who like to talk about things like what necktie they wore to Alberto Ascari's funeral. And in the second place, they won't let me drive drunk. They expect me to go out there and smash into things and roll over on the roof and catch fire and burn to death when I'm sober. They must think I'm crazy. That stuff scares me. I have to get completely shit-faced to even think about driving fast. How can you have a lot of exciting thrills when you're so terrified that you wet yourself all the time? That's not fun. It's just *not fun* to have exciting thrills when you're scared. Take the heroes of the *Iliad,* for instance—they really had some exciting thrills, and were they scared? No. They were drunk. Every chance they could get. And so am I, and I'm not going out there and have a horrible car wreck until somebody brings me a cocktail.

Also, it's important to be drunk because being drunk keeps your body all loose, and that way, if you have an accident or anything, you'll sort of roll with the punches and not get banged up so bad. For example, there was this guy I heard about who was really drunk and was driving through the Adirondacks. He got sideswiped by a bus and went head-on into another car, which knocked him off a bridge, and he plummeted 150 feet into a ravine. I mean, it killed him and everything, but if he hadn't been so drunk and loose, his body probably would have been banged up a lot worse—and you can imagine how much more upset his wife would have been when she went down to the morgue to identify him.

Even more important than being drunk, however, is having the right car. You have to get a car that handles really well. This is extremely important, and there's a lot of debate on this subject —about what kind of car handles best. Some say a front-engined car; some say a rear-engined car. I say a *rented* car. Nothing handles better than a rented car. You can go faster, turn corners sharper, and put the transmission into reverse while going forward at a higher rate of speed in a rented car than in any other kind. You can also park without looking, and can use the trunk as an ice chest. Another thing about a rented car is that it's an all-terrain vehicle. Mud, snow, water, woods—you can take a rented car anywhere. True, you can't always get it back—but that's not your problem, is it?

P. J. O'Rourke

Yet there's more to a really good-handling car than just making sure it doesn't belong to you. It has to be big. It's really hard for a girl to get her clothes off inside a small car, and this is one of the most important features of car handling. Also, what kind of drugs does it have in it? Most people like to drive on speed or cocaine with plenty of whiskey mixed in. This gives you the confidence you want and need for plowing through red lights and passing trucks on the right. But don't neglect downs and 'ludes and codeine cough syrup either. It's hard to beat the heavy depressants for high-speed spin-outs, backing into trees, and a general feeling of not giving two fucks about man and his universe.

Overall, though, it's the bigness of the car that counts the most. Because when something bad happens in a really big car—accidentally speeding through the middle of a gang of unruly young people who have been taunting you in a drive-in restaurant, for instance—it happens very far away—way out at the end of your fenders. It's like a civil war in Africa; you know, it doesn't really concern you too much. On the other hand, when something happens in a little bitty car it happens right in your face. You get all involved in it and have to give everything a lot of thought. Driving around in a little bitty car is like being one of those sensitive girls who writes poetry. Life is just too much to bear. You end up staying at home in your bedroom and thinking up sonnets that don't get published till you die, which will be real soon if you keep driving around in little bitty cars like that.

Let's inspect some of the basic maneuvers of drunken driving while you've got crazy girls who are on drugs with you. Look for these signs when picking up crazy girls: pierced ears with five or six earrings in them, unusual shoes, white lipstick, extreme thinness, hair that's less than an inch long, or clothing made of chrome and leather. Stay away from girls who cry a lot or who look like they get pregnant easily or have careers. They may want to do weird stuff in cars, but only in the backseat, and it's really hard to steer from back there. Besides, they'll want to get engaged right away afterwards. But the other kind of girls—there's no telling what they'll do. I used to know this girl who weighed about eighty pounds and dressed in skirts that didn't even cover her underwear, when she wore any. I had this beat-up old Mercedes, and we were off someplace about fifty miles from nowhere on Christmas Eve in a horrible sleetstorm. The road was really a mess, all curves and big ditches, and I was blotto, and the car kept slipping off the pavement and sliding sideways. And just when I'd hit a big patch of glare ice and was frantically spinning the wheel trying to stay out of the oncoming traffic, she said, "I shaved my crotch today— wanna feel?"

That's really true. And then about half an hour later the head gasket blew up, and we had to spend I don't know how long in this dirtball motel, although the girl walked all the way to the liquor store through about a mile of slush and got all kinds of wine and did weird stuff with the bottlenecks later. So it was sort of okay, except that the garage where I left the Mercedes burned down and I used the insurance money to buy a motorcycle.

Now, girls who like motorcycles really will do *anything*. I mean, really, *anything you can think of*. But it's just not the same. For one thing, it's hard to drink while you're riding a motorcycle —there's no place to set your glass. And cocaine's out of the question. And personally, I find that grass makes me too sensitive. You smoke some grass and the first thing you know you're pulling over to the side of the road and taking a break to dig the gentle beauty of the sky's vast panorama, the slow, luxurious interlay of sun and clouds, the lulling trill of breezes midst leafy tree branches —and what kind of fun is that? Besides, it's tough to "get it on" with a chick (I mean in the biblical sense) and still make all the fast curves unless you let her take the handlebars with her pants off and come on doggy-style or something, which is harder than it sounds; and pantless girls on motorcycles attract the highway patrol, so usually you don't end up doing anything until you're both off the bike, and by then you may be in the hospital. Like I was after this old lady pulled out in front of me in an Oldsmobile, and the girl I was with still wanted to do anything you can think of, but there was a doctor there and he was squirting pHisoHex all over me and combing little bits of gravel out of my face with a wire brush, and I just couldn't get into it. So take it from me and don't get a motorcycle. Get a big car.

Usually, most fast-driving maneuvers that don't require crazy girls call for use of the steering wheel, so be sure your car is equipped with power steering. Without power steering, turning the wheel is a lot like work, and if you wanted work you'd get a job. All steering should be done with the index finger. Then, when you're done doing all the steering that you want to do, just pull your finger out of there and the wheel will come right back to wherever it wants to. It's that simple. Be sure to do an extra lot of steering when going into a driveway or turning sharp corners. And here's another important tip: Always roll the window down before throwing bottles out, and don't try to throw them through the windshield unless the car is parked.

Okay, now say you've been on a six-day drunk and you've just made a bet that you can back up all the way to Cleveland, plus you've got a buddy who's getting a blow job on the trunk lid. Well, let's face it—if that's the way you're going to act, sooner or later you'll have an accident. This much is true. But that doesn't mean that you should sit back and just let accidents happen to you. No, you have to go out and cause them yourself. That way you're in control of the situation.

You know, it's a shame, but a lot of people have the wrong idea about accidents. For one thing, they don't hurt nearly as much as you'd think. That's because you're in shock and can't feel pain, or if you aren't in shock, you're dead, and that doesn't hurt at all so far as we know. Another thing is that they make great stories. I've got this friend—a prominent man in the automotive industry —who flipped his MG TF back in the fifties and slid on his head for a couple hundred yards, and had to spend a year with no eyelids and a steel pin through his cheekbones while his face was being rebuilt. Sure, it wasn't much fun at the time, but you should hear him tell about it now. What a fabulous tale, especially during dinner. Besides, it's not all smashing glass and spurting blood, you understand. Why, a good sideswipe can be an almost religious experience. The sheet metal doesn't break or crunch or anything —it flexes and gives way as the two vehicles come together with a rushing liquid pulse as if two giant sharks of steel were mating in the perpetual night of the sea primordial. I mean, if you're on enough drugs. Also, sometimes you see a lot of really pretty lights in your head.

One sure way to cause an accident is with your basic "moonshiner's" or "bootlegger's" turn. Whiz down the road at about sixty or seventy, throw the gearshift into neutral, cut the wheel to the left, and hit the emergency brake with one good wallop while holding the brake release out with your left hand. This'll send you spinning around in a perfect 180-degree turn right into a culvert or a fast-moving tractor-trailer rig. (The bootlegger's turn can be done on dry pavement, but it works best on top of loose gravel or small children.) Or, when you've moved around backwards, you can then spin the wheel to the right and keep on going until you've come around a full 360 degrees and are headed back the same way you were going; though it probably would have been easier to have just kept going that way in the first place and not have done anything at all, unless you were with somebody you really wanted to impress—your probation officer, for instance.

An old friend of mine named Joe Schenkman happens to have just written me a letter about another thing you can do to wreck a car. Joe's on a little vacation up in Vermont (and will be until he finds out what the statute of limitations on attempted vehicular homicide is). He was writing to tell me about a fellow he met up there, saying:

> . . . This guy has rolled (deliberately) over thirty cars (and not
> just by his own account—the townfolks back him up on this
> story), inheriting only a broken nose (three times) and a
> slightly black-and-blue shoulder for all this. What you do,

see, is you go into a moonshiner's turn, but you get on the brakes and stay on them. Depending on how fast you're going, you roll proportionately; four or five rolls is decent. Going into the spin, you have one hand on the seat and the other firmly on the roof so you're sprung in tight. As you feel the roof give on the first roll, you slip your seat hand under the dash (of the passenger side, as you're thrown hard over in that direction to begin with) and pull yourself under it. And here you simply sit it out, springing yourself tight with your whole body, waiting for the thunder to die. Naturally, it helps to be drunk, and if you have a split second's doubt or hesitation through any of this, you die.

This Schenkman himself is no slouch of a driver, I may say. Unfortunately, his strong suit is driving in New York City, an area that has a great number of unusual special conditions, which we just don't have the time or the space to get into right here (except to note that the good part is how it's real easy to scare old ladies in new Cadillacs and the bad part is that Negroes actually *do* carry knives, not to mention Puerto Ricans; and everybody else you hit turns out to be a lawyer or married to somebody in the mob). However, Joe is originally from the South, and it was down there that he discovered huffing glue and sniffing industrial solvents and such. These give you a really spectacular hallucinatory type of a high where you think, for instance, that you're driving through an overpass guardrail and landing on a freight-train flatcar and being hauled to Shreveport and loaded into a container ship headed for Liberia with a crew full of homosexual Lebanese, only to come to and find out that it's true. Joe is a commercial artist who enjoys jazz music and horse racing. His favorite color is blue.

There's been a lot of discussion about what kind of music to listen to while staring doom square in the eye and not blinking unless you get some grit under your contacts. Watch out for the fellow who tunes his FM to the classical station. He thinks a little

Republican Party Reptile

Rimsky-Korsakov makes things more dramatic—like in a foreign movie. That's pussy style. This kind of guy's idea of a fast drive is a seventy-five-mile-an-hour cruise up to the summer cottage after one brandy and soda. The true skidmark artist prefers something cheery and upbeat—"Night on Disco Mountain" or "Boogie Oogie Oogie" or whatever it is that the teenage lovely wants to shake her buns to. Remember her? So what do *you* care what's on the fucking tape deck? The high, hot whine of the engine, the throaty pitch of the exhaust, the wind in your beer can, the gentle slurping noises from her little bud-red lips—that's all the music your ears need, although side two of the first Velvet Underground album is nice if you absolutely insist. And no short jaunts either. For the maniacal high-speed driver, endurance is everything. Especially if you've used that ever-popular pickup line "Wanna go to Mexico?" Especially if you've used it somewhere like Boston. Besides, teenage girls can go a long, long time without sleep, and believe me, so can the police and their parents. So just keep your foot in it. There's no reason not to. There's no reason not to keep going forever, really. I had this friend who drove a whole shitload of people up from Oaxaca to Cincinnati one time, nonstop. I mean, he stopped for gas but he wouldn't even let anybody get out then. He made them all piss out the windows, and he says that it was worth the entire drive just to *see* a girl try to piss out the window of a moving car.

Get a fat girl friend so you'll have plenty of amphetamines and you'll never have to stop at all. The only problem you'll run into is that after you've been driving for two or three days you start to see things in the road—great big scaly things twenty feet high with nine legs. But there are very few great big scaly things with nine legs in America anymore, so you can just drive right through them because they probably aren't really there, and if they *are* really there you'll be doing the country a favor by running them over.

Yes, but where does it all end? Where does a crazy life like this lead? To death, you say. Look at all the people who've died

136

in car wrecks: Albert Camus, Jayne Mansfield, Jackson Pollock, Tom Paine. Well, Tom Paine didn't *really* die in a car wreck, but he probably would have if he'd lived a little later. He was that kind of guy. Anyway, death is always the first thing that leaps into everybody's mind—sudden violent death at an early age. If only it were that simple. God, we could all go out in a blaze of flaming aluminum alloys formulated specially for the Porsche factory race effort like James Dean did! No ulcers, no hemorrhoids, no bulging waistlines, soft dicks, or false teeth . . . *bash!! kaboom!! Watch this space for paperback reprint rights, auction, and movie option sale!* But that's not the way it goes. No. What actually happens is you fall for that teenage lovely in the next seat over, fall for her like a ton of condoms, and before you know it you're married and have teenage lovelies of your own—getting felt up in a Pontiac Trans Ams this very minute, no doubt—plus a six-figure mortgage, a liver the size of the Bronx, and a Country Squire that's never seen the sweet side of sixty.

It's hard to face the truth, but I suppose you yourself realize that if you'd had just a little more courage, just a little more strength of character, you could have been dead by now. No such luck.

Manners
and Mores

Hollywood
Etiquette

~~~~~~

"Hollywood" is not, of course, a place. Nor is it a synonym for the entertainment business. There are upstanding citizens who make their living in that field. The real Hollywood is the *reductio ad absurdum* of personal liberty. It is ordinary men and women freed by money and social mobility to do anything they want unencumbered by family pressure, community mores, social responsibility, civic duty, or good sense. There's a little streak of it in us all.

The entertainment business is a venue for Hollywood because heaps of money can be made by entertaining and because the public is famously tolerant of entertainers. Los Angeles is a site for Hollywood because, if all the freedom and money go blooey, it's warm enough to sleep on the beach. Other places and professions have had this distinction at other times. During the eighteenth century it was the pirate nests of the Caribbean. When the Medici popes were in office, it was the College of Cardinals.

It is interesting that when people have great resources and few restraints they don't always run amok doing evil to their fellow man. In Hollywood the evil is mostly self-destructive. On the other hand the good is limited to an occasional movie like *Tender Mercies.* Thus Hollywood is a disappointment to Hobbes conservatives and Rousseau liberals alike. But it is fascinating to the student of manners.

Manners are the formal and ceremonial manifestations of a society's underlying values. Usually these values are things like loyalty, altruism, veneration of the elderly, valor, etc. But what sort of manners emerge in a society such as Hollywood's where the only underlying value is personal gratification? The answer is none. Friends are ignored. Enemies and chance acquaintances are greeted with kisses. People meet in public places to discuss finance before breakfast. Total strangers ask you what you paid for your shoes.

It's hard for a visitor from the civilized world to detect any standards at all. People shout the details of their sexual lives but conceal with embarrassment the brand of car they own. The streets are lined with expensive clothing stores, but no one dresses up. Restaurants have unlisted phone numbers. You never know what the natives are going to do next.

Not only the rich and irresponsible act this way but also the would-be rich and the would-be irresponsible. Feckless eccentricity has spread to every level of society, especially in the service industries. Waiters introduce themselves by name, inquire into your home life, and, if you aren't careful, will invite themselves to sit down and sample your wine choice. At the grocery store, when you extend a palm for change you're liable to have your Line of Life and Mountain of Venus examined and longevity foretold by the number of wrinkles around your wrist. Policemen pull you over for traffic infractions and show you résumés and 8×10 glossies.

A strong element of fantasy must be allowed for in Hollywood behavior. It can be disconcerting to do business with a bank officer in jogging shorts who does deep knee bends while discussing variable-rate mortgages. Meanwhile the man who cleans the pool comes around in a Cardin suit. The owner of every commercial establishment seems lost in dreams of grandeur. The drive-in restaurant has valet parking.

But sometimes Hollywood is too normal. Bellhops salute and carry eight bags without complaint. Taxi drivers tip their caps and say "You're the boss" when you tell them to go to Bel Air from Santa Monica by way of Sherman Oaks. It takes a while to realize what's going on. The bellhops and taxi drivers are *acting*. They're engaged in that rarest kind of fantasy life, imagining reality is real. Don't expect an encore, however. Tomorrow they'll be surly, drug-addicted rock stars.

Though there are no standards of behavior in Hollywood, there are some criteria of status: money, power, and fame. Money —though it is the first cause, prime mover, and only useful product of Hollywood—is the least important. Hollywood is a single-crop economy, and there's just too much money around. Millions are paid for Benedict Canyon building lots 2 degrees shy of vertical. Olympic-size swimming pools are built for families who haven't been outdoors since 1965. People send their pets to psychiatrists. Everyone has money or spends it as if he did. (Though there's no idea of what money might do. A fortune Joseph P. Kennedy would have used to elect a new Senate is spent on wristwatches.)

Money being common, prestige goes instead to power. There's endless talk about power in Hollywood and much deference paid to it. But it's a silly kind of puissance. What would Talleyrand have made of someone who had the power to put *Leave It to Beaver* back on network television or the power to turn a popular soft-drink jingle into a $30 million movie staring Lorna Luft? As for real power—the force to direct events and guide human affairs—the people of Hollywood don't seem to have that over even their own lives.

Since money is hackneyed and power is trivial, the real gauge of Hollywood status is fame. People are introduced in terms of their fame, even if they don't have any: "This is Heather. She would have been on *Good Morning America* if Andropov hadn't died that day." Fame is so important that the slightest association with it confers standing: "I'd like you to meet Trevor. His sister-in-law goes to the same chiropractor as Bo Derek's aunt." Even physical proximity to fame will do: "Wayne here lives three blocks away from Sonny Bono."

Fame of one's own is best, of course, but it's strictly quantitative. Any kind of fame will do. A lesser-known Supreme Court justice, the woman who tried to shoot Gerald Ford, and the actor who played Timmy on the *Lassie* TV show are about equal.

If absolutely no fame or any association with it can be mustered, then singularity will do. The people of Hollywood put immense effort into making themselves unusual. This isn't easy in a world where being normal is the next worst thing to being pale and fat. Half a dozen *soi-disant* actresses may show up at a party in identical skunk-striped pedal pushers, yellow rain slickers, and antique corsets worn as blouses. In the last resort, Hollywood people buy strange automobiles and show you a 1962 pink Cadillac limousine with a baby grand piano built into the backseat. "It's the only one like it," they'll say. True, thank God.

With no values larger than the self, no sensible norms, no meaningful pecking order, and no fixed goals or objectives except attracting attention, Hollywood is a place of confusion. Play is confused with work and duty with employment so that a $50 million stock issue, a tennis match, and a dangerously ill mother are all greeted with the same mixture of frantic worry and stupid enthusiasm. Hollywood people often get themselves in financial trouble because they forget that spending thirty hours a week at a Nautilus gym is difficult, but no one will pay you to do it.

Confusion reigns in every aspect of existence. Romance is remarkably muddled. Sex is confused with love. Love is confused with marriage. People not only go to bed on a first date but discuss business there. Couples don't stay wed long enough to get to know each other. Child-rearing is muzzy in the extreme. Children are mistaken for friends or, sometimes, possessions. Often there seems to be a casting call for baby in the house. Who will get the part? Will it be Mom? Mom's third husband? Or the baby? There is even spatial confusion in Hollywood. Practically everyone runs or jogs. Then he gets in the car to go next door.

No distinction is made between private and public life. All talk, even to the dogs, is about money, power, and fame. Or it would be if anyone's attention span were long enough. Hollywood conversations are disconcerting things to overhear.

Producer A: "We paid a million five for our house."

Screenwriter B: "Did anybody get fired at Universal Studios today?"

A: "Cher dyed her hair green."

B: "What did that Rolex cost you?"

A: "I just signed to do a sequel to *Rhinestone.*"

B: "We paid a million three for our place in Palm Springs."

Even Hollywood people can't keep this up for long without going nuts. As a result, talking on the telephone has replaced real conversation. Not that you ever talk to the person you called. There are too many answering machines, answering services, call-waiting features, multiple lines, and extension phones in peculiar places like the car trunk. And whoever you called is always on the phone already anyway. Instead you have long, intimate talks with the decorator, the Mexican gardener, the secretary, the nanny, or, most often, a phone repairman. This and cute recorded messages is how Hollywood people stay in touch. And stay in touch they must. No one in Hollywood is secure enough to spend five minutes alone with his thoughts.

Hollywood people are insecure about their taste, about their intellect, about themselves. And they should be.

Taste cannot function in such an environment because taste is contextual. Taste is the appropriate thing, and nothing can be appropriate to everything and nothing at once. A Hollywood individual may have a sense of style, but it's a loose cannon on the deck. When you drive through Beverly Hills you see grand Spanish haciendas with English lawns, charming French chateaus with attached garages, stately Tudor manses with palm trees and cactus gardens, all built right next to each other on dopey suburban lots. The owners could afford vast estates except they're ignorant of nature. They could own elegant townhouses but there's no town to put them in. Instead they live in a World's Fair of motley home styles divorced from natural setting and human community alike.

The intellect cannot function in such an environment. The mind doesn't work without order and rank. Thus Hollywood people can hardly think. And when they do think, they think the strangest things:

"The Grenada invasion must have been wrong because no one has written a best-seller about it yet."

"A lot of people think it was just Robert Redford, but if it hadn't been for Dustin Hoffman there never would have been a Watergate exposé."

When had at all, intelligence tends, like fame, to be quantitative. Ask someone if a record album is good, and he'll give you its position on the *Billboard* Top 100 chart. Ask someone how his six-year-old daughter is, he'll tell you her IQ.

In Hollywood the smallest exercise of the mental faculties becomes a Sisyphean task. You'll be standing in line at a movie theater and the ticket seller will ask the person in front of you, "How many?"

"Oh, wow," comes the response. "There's, you know, me. That's one. Then there's this woman I'm with. I mean, I'm not really with her. We both see other people. But, like, we're together tonight except we don't know whether our relationship is growing or not. So there's her. That's two. And then there are these friends of ours. But they didn't make it . . . ."

In fact, the human soul cannot function in such an environment.

P. J. O'Rourke

There is general agreement that primitive societies are valuable resources. Mankind benefits in understanding and knowledge from the preservation of native cultures. But I don't think any ethical social scientist would object if we got rid of this one.

Dinner-Table
Conversation

~~~~~~

The Book of Proverbs says, "Better is a dinner of herbs where love is, than a stalled ox and hatred therewith." But a dinner with brilliant conversation surpasses herbs, ox, and love combined. The best pleasures of the feast proceed from the lips, not to them.

As a scene for conversation, dinner has great advantages. The company is gathered closely together. Interruptions are discouraged. And performing one of the few pleasant bodily functions sets a happy mood. Also, there is another use available for the mouth. This is important. Statements and responses may be composed while teeth glean the inside of an artichoke leaf, while a bite of something more substantial yields respite when you've chatted your way into a cul-de-sac. And a drink of wine loosens the expressive tongue and reins the critical ear. The only better place for conversation is bed. But unless you have ultramodern standards, that limits the guest list. And even then, having five or six people in your bed is more likely to cause talk than conversation.

Any kind of dinner is not sufficient, however. A tea or buffet won't do. It may be an indication of today's Freudian obsessions, but few modern people can talk with anything in their laps. Dinner must be a sit-down meal. And the number of guests must be small, seven at most. Conversation is not a spectator sport or a relay race to be run up and down a banquet table seating fifty. There should be no visual obstructions such as immense floral centerpieces. It is impossible for a guest to make any but the most pastoral repartee when his face is framed in mums. Also, the food has to be of a kind which allows one guest to look another in the face while eating. Corn on the cob is bad. Spaghetti is worse. French onion soup is unthinkable. Emphasize refreshments. The better the wine, champagne, and brandy, the stronger and brighter the talk. Eschew the guest who doesn't drink. He's too likely to talk about why he doesn't. Also avoid hard liquor. The grape evokes the muses. But there is something in spirits distilled from grain that brings forth domestic animals. Gin martinis are particularly dangerous. Guests are reduced to dogs in their communicative abilities—sniffing and nipping at each other and raising the hair on the napes of their necks. The best way to beg off serving martinis is to keep only the worst brands of sweet vermouth in your house.

Of course, the guests must be carefully selected. Mix good talkers with good listeners. And don't confuse good listeners with people who are simply quiet. Furniture is quiet. A good listener listens with enthusiasm. He encourages the talker, asks pertinent questions, is able to expand upon the subject or deftly change it if the talk has become monochromatic. A good talker must have all the qualities of a good listener plus an ability to hold forth at length: to tell a fully rounded anecdote, make an elaborate jest, convey news in piquant detail, or give an unexpected coif to the feathers of reason. And a good talker must be able to do this without inspiring other guests to pitch him out a window. Such people are invaluable. They give the rest of us time to eat.

Republican Party Reptile

Conversation is a group activity, and the participants should be thought of as a team, albeit with certain stars. The best teamwork is the result of practice. The best guests for good conversation are guests who've had good conversation with each other before. Their moves are polished. Mr. X will give lavish praise to some item of popular culture and pass the ball to Miss Y, who will say something pert.

Mr. X: "*Smithereens* is an artfully unattractive movie with a protagonist who's purposely unsympathetic, and it has no scenes showing development of personal relationships because our imaginations are intended to fill in not what happened but what did not."

Miss Y: "Things which require more than three negatives to praise never make money."

The wit of the Algonquin round table had more to do with such drill than with the native genius of its habitués.

If you can't invite the same group repeatedly or if you don't know any such group to invite, then try to gather people who have something in common. But make sure what they have in common is not a point of vanity. Only an idiot would have two sports impresarios, two opera tenors, or two Supreme Court justices at the table.

Also make sure your guests don't want to kill each other—a warning that should be unnecessary. But many hosts think it "interesting" to invite to the same fête, say, the head of a PLO faction and the prime minister of Israel or Norman Mailer and all his ex-wives. This is all right for cocktail parties, but at a small seated dinner it's liable to result in stony silences or tossed gravy boats.

And do not invite people who have only one interest in their lives even if everyone else at the meal is similarly obsessed. Extended conversations on one topic quickly degenerate from ideas to opinions and from opinions to bigotries. Six fervent devotees of French Symbolist poetry will be fine through soup, but by cheese and fruit they will be yelling at each other.

"Verlaine's clustered images suggesting mood and emotion stink like pigs!"

"Do not!"

And so on.

The one thing which has to be mutual among guests is not acquaintance, interests, or background but attitude. Good conversation takes place on a plane above mortal affairs. There must be sufficient detachment to banish the stupider emotions. The purpose of conversation—if something that's so much an art can be said to have a purpose—is to learn how others see things, how others make sense of existence or make peace with its nonsensicality. Good conversation gives you the advantage of being Argus-eyed or Hydra-headed (though, it is to be hoped, with nicer heads).

Conversation is therefore no place to talk about yourself. Your guests can observe *you* perfectly well and don't need help. What they want to hear is something they don't know or haven't thought of. Conversation is especially no place for the small and boring extensions of the self. Do not talk about your pets or infant grandchildren. By the same token, avoid being too personal with others. Some will think your inquiries rude, but, worse, the rest will jump to answer them. The disease of narcissism is not cured by spreading it around the table.

Neither has conversation room for awe or envy. Someone may be admired or praised, but an awestruck recitation of the powers and virtues of Fritz Mondale, for example, would put a damper on the evening. And a sudden outburst of jealous indignation that you aren't he would bring talk to a shocked halt.

Bitterness and complaint also lower the tone of conversation, and violate a rule of general decorum besides: "A gentleman never complains about anything he is unable or unwilling to remedy." Unless you're going to dash from the table and balance Social Security's income and outlay with a personal check, you should have another glass of wine and let the talk pass to outrageous defense expenditures.

Republican Party Reptile

The taboo against querulousness, however, should not be taken as a prohibition of damning things. Damning is a perfectly Olympian thing to do and has been a source of delight to great minds throughout history. You can damn the government up and down, call its every minion illegitimate progeny of slime mold, and say that a visit to Washington is like taking a bath in a tub full of live squid, so long as you don't complain.

An attitude of egalitarianism is necessary, as well as an attitude of detachment. There is an unwritten law of dinner table democracy. No matter how famous and powerful some guests or how humble and obscure others, they're all equal when they sit down to eat. Thus there should be no overt aggression or competitiveness. Evangelizing, pontification, and the telling of jokes are all wrong. An attempt to convert and an assumption of omniscience are both competitive acts. And a joke is a rhetorical device that renders the teller dominant and the listener submissive. If a joke is so appropriate to the conversation that you have to tell it, turn the joke into an anecdote.

If, for instance, the talk is about political oppression in Eastern Europe, tell how Czech dissidents have a joke about a shopper who stands in line at a butcher store for fifteen hours only to be told there is no meat. When he complains loudly, a trench-coated stranger steps out of the crowd. "Comrade," whispers the stranger, "control yourself. In the old days if a person complained like that, well . . ." The stranger makes a pistol gesture with his fingers.

The shopper returns home. When his wife sees he's empty-handed, she asks, "What's the matter, are they out of meat?"

"Worse than that," replies the shopper. "They're out of bullets."

This joke was told in political cabaret skits in Prague before the 1968 Russian invasion. By saying so you remove the onus of telling a joke directly. Otherwise you're attempting conversational bondage and discipline.

More obnoxious than a joke is a heated debate. Not only is it aggressive, but it violates the spirit of conversation as an art form.

P. J. O'Rourke

A conversation is not expected to "decide something" any more than a painting by Matisse is.

And most repulsive of all faults in parlance is advice. It shows every kind of disrespect for the knowledge and judgment of others and combines that with an exhibit of gross lack of common sense in the purveyor. What's never taken should be never offered.

If the attitudes are right then there is no such thing as a wrong subject. Even grandchildren can be discussed if you have adequate detachment to sketch them as the little beasts they are. But, generally, the subjects of conversation fall into three categories: ideas, information, and gossip.

Ideas may be distinguished from their duller cousins, opinions, in that ideas are living things which may be pruned, grafted onto, or forced to blossom as they pass around the table, whereas opinions are dead sticks most often used in thrashing equally dead equines. "Meryl Streep is able to portray a sexuality that goes beyond the confines of prurience." That's an idea. "Meryl Streep is real good." That's an opinion. Stick to ideas. They're, well, less opinionated-sounding.

Information is something everyone desires and no one has the patience to endure receiving. Who has not suffered an explanation of how pork-belly futures work? But any information can be fascinating if properly conveyed. There is a biochemist in New York who is able to explain cell meiosis in terms of high school romance: how DNA breaks apart the same way a teenager hates to spend time with her family and how that teenage bundle of chromosomes meets up with some cute DNA that moved in next door on a sperm. Then the two of them hook up and start the whole biological ranch house with one and a half baths and a carport all over again. The key is in keeping your terms and concepts general. Avoid jargon. Few computer experts would care to be addressed in Swahili, yet the same experts confound their listeners with bytes, floppy disks, and core dumps.

Gossip is everyone's favorite subject. Of course, gossip is terrible. But so are all of us. No one is going to stop gossiping, so you might as well do it right. Never gossip about people you don't know. This is stealing bread from the mouths of simple artisans such as Suzy or Rona Barrett. Also, it gives others the impression that the people you do know are a pretty dull lot. Announce your gossip with a straight face. Sophistication does not admit to surprise, and knowledge of human nature should preclude disappointment. And present all scandals in a forthright and unexaggerated form. Some degree of honesty must be present in conversation or it lapses into a lower form of art such as literature.

Good conversation may be thought assured by lively people, smart attitudes, and topics sufficiently worthwhile or sufficiently otherwise. But anything can be spoiled by technique.

There must be a rhythm of exchange among the guests. Everyone must make a contribution even if that contribution is only a pretended inability to swallow a mouthful of soup because of the stunning nature of what's been said. No one should ever be excluded. Nothing is more disgusting than five people talking intimately about something a sixth person has never heard of. You might as well invite that person to dinner and not serve him food. There should be no extended duets unless only two people are present. You should have no honeymoon couples (marital, commercial, or other) at your table. And there should be no seductions evident. Flirtations may be rampant, but they should be public and tend to the amusement, or astonishment anyway, of the whole company.

Ideally one guest should have a say; there should be general response; the first guest should make rebuttal or retraction; and the floor should pass to someone else. When it does so, the subject should also change at least slightly. Francis Bacon, in his seventeenth-century essay "Of Discourse," said, "The honourablest part of talk is to give the occasion; and again to moderate and pass to somewhat else; for then a man leads the dance."

Changes of tone and style should be as frequent as changes of speaker and subject. Anecdote should not pile on anecdote but be mixed with observation, quip, hypothesis, question, etc. This is not just for the sake of variety. In conversation, unlike bridge, it's bad taste to follow suit. If Miss A mentions that she knows an actress with 240 pairs of shoes, only a beast would let on that he's met a countess who owns three hundred. It is your duty as host to mitigate such trespasses. You have to say something to the effect of "Yes, the countess does own three hundred pairs of shoes. But her father was so impoverished by European tax laws that he was forced to marry a wealthy insect, and therefore the lady in question has six feet."

It is, in fact, your duty to see to the smooth running of all conversational machinery. In a perfect situation, this means nothing but keeping the glasses full. But usually you also need to curtail monopolization by the skilled, solicit participation from the dull, and excuse that participation to the spirited. You must dress nettled pride with compliments, perform oral surgery to remove people's feet from their mouths, and, if argument gets completely out of hand, pretend the maid just had a baby in the kitchen.

Remember that trick. You're also the person who will eventually have to make everyone shut up and go home.

An Alphabet for Schoolboys

*Consisting of simple
verses replete with sound
advice on manners and
learning and
admonishments both
moral and otherwise*

~~~~~~

A is for Algebra, thoroughgoing bore.
To pass it is asked you, no less and no more.
For though algebra's dreary, complex, and abstruse,
Thank God, out of school, it's of no further use.

B is for Beer. It makes you act lewd
And stupid and loud. It's a ruinous fluid
For people with taste, for people who think.
Beer is not nice. It's a bad thing to drink.
The consumption of beer is low-class and risky.
Stick to gin, vodka, cocaine, and whiskey.

C is the mark you should always have made.
It's a simple and forthright and manly-type grade.

P. J. O'Rourke

For an "A" gives your peer group sad indication
Of a social life lacking inspiration,
While "B" is overreaching for most humankind,
Yet displays lassitude in the genius mind,
And "D" is the sign of a mental defective,
And "F" invites violent parental invective.
"C" is the best. It shows moderation,
The goal of philosophers in each age and nation.

D is for Drugs, that's to say, marijuana.
A most common flora with your age of fauna.
This herb is mind-widening; it improves your
    perspective,
And makes you intuitive, kind, and perceptive.
It heightens your senses, sets your psyche free,
Causes you to care for ecology,
And imbues you with other qualities that
Let people sneak up and crap in your hat.

E is for Effort. Never let it show.
If you look like you're trying, people will know
That you have aspirations, that you are ambitious.
They'll consider you dangerous, pushy, malicious.
Traditional society is not forgiving
Of the upwardly mobile. They're made to work for a
    living.

F is for Failure, a horrible curse.
Success is the only thing known that is worse.
People like goof-offs, losers, and quitters.
Towards champions and victors they feel little but bitter.
Pretend you succeeded and say that you spurned it.
But if you succeed, don't let on that you earned it.
There's something for which folks have more hate
    reserv'd

Than for chance success. It's success
deserv'd.

G is for solid Geometry
Which mystifies you as it mystified me.
So much so, in fact, I'm afraid I'm not deft
Enough to go rhyme it. I'll make another rhyme on *F*:
F is for Fun—toot-toot! beep-beep!
Have it all now. It doesn't keep.

H is for Hard-ons, erections in your pants,
During gym, in the lunch line, and at the Y dance.
Don't blush, don't blow off your head with a Mauser
Because of the rude bulging tent in your trousers.
Just wait, relax, thirty years from this fall
You'll feel total elation to have one at all.

I stands for Integration, interethnical mix,
Where busing gives society's inequities the fix.
Don't slug your new schoolmate or whack his nappy
dome.
Don't slap him or tease him or arson his home.
Cheer him instead on field, in gym, at race,
And win money bet on his oddly hued face.

J is for Jack-off, a.k.a. masturbation.
Do it each school night and twice on vacation.
It's much less expensive than what you do with your
dick
When you're grown up—as you will find all too quick.

K is for Kleenex suffused with your love.
(*Vid.* poem for *J* directly above.)

P. J. O'Rourke

L is for Latin, a language so peaked
Even the Romans of yore do not speak it.
If you don't believe what I say, go see
Reruns of *I, Claudius* from the BBC.

M is for "Most Popular," also "Best Dressed,"
"Best Dancer," "Cutest Couple," and all of the rest.
The sleek cheerleader, the lead in the class play—
She'll wind up fat; he'll turn out gay.
The boy who's presently a football star,
In a dozen years will sell used cars.
The girl who's now the Homecoming Queen,
She'll end her days divorced in Moline.
Half of her court will be bottomless dancers.
The class stud will die of testicular cancers.
While the Student Council President
Will be an Ashram resident.
And for the sake of mercy there should be a UN
    moratorium
On the kind of things that happen to the earnest
    valedictorian.
Remember, the future visits every duress
On the victims of adolescent success.
Besides, so what if you aren't a social lion?
Neither was Zola nor Albert Einstein.

N is for Nike. It's a missile not a shoe.
Get yourself an oxford in cordovan, not blue.

O is for Offal, served in the cafeteria.
Regard it as you would a vaccination for diphtheria.
Lunchroom food is made in order to prepare you
For the treatment you'll receive from the girl who will
    marry you,

And for military, business, and personal strife,
And the rest of the shit you'll eat later in life.

P is for Prom night, most important by far
If you enjoy vomit and hand jobs in cars.
It's a night no sensible person would fail
To forget, with exception of one small detail:
The pictures your parents are sure to have took*
Which they'll frame and hang in the vestibule nook.
This picture will publish in all the newspapers
If you have a car wreck or become a child raper.
So be sure your tuxedo is plain and fits right
And looks as though owned and not hired that night,
And be sure that your hair is properly plastered
To your skull like a man's, not a hippy disaster's
(Nor parted in the middle like a local sportscaster's).
This photo may get international play,
Depending on what you do or you say.
And you don't want the world to think you a loon
If you happen to die or shoot the President soon.

*There is absolutely no excusage
For this past participle usage.*

Q is for Questions of every kind,
The sign of an unwell and feverish mind.
Don't succumb to the ill of curiosities.
The cure is worse always than the disease.
He's only more worried, he who knows.
For your peace of mind let me propose
The motto immemorial of the Bengal Lancers:
"Don't ask questions. You'll only get answers."

R is for Rah-rah, rah-rah, rah-rah,
Boom-a-lacka, boom-a-lacka, sis, boom, bah.

Control yourself, remain demure.
School spirit is fearfully immature.
Your high school fight song will strike a false note
When you're older and pretending you went off to
Choate.

S is for Scholastic Aptitude Test.
Be sure to do better than all of the rest.
That way you'll get into Harvard or Yale,
And land a job in the government if you pass or you
fail.
And government is a lucrative field
With loads of influence and power to wield.
Plus a government job insures that eventually,
When you're caught, you'll serve time in the best
penitentiary.

T is for Tender kind charity.
Work hard at getting rich if you ever want to see
Any of it. Since charity is most felicitous
When its object is rich to the point of conspicuousness.

U is for the Unemployment rates,
Still rather grim in most cities and states.
There may be no jobs no matter what your knowledge,
By the time that you matriculate from college.
So work and study and practice night and day
At something to give you social entrée.
There may be no jobs, not for doctor nor dentist,
But you'll marry an heiress if you're real good at tennis.

V is for Verse, all adolescents write,
Mawkish, self-pitying, derivative, trite.
But at least, today, all verse is free,
So verse is easier than it used to be.

For poems once were written in doggerel thus:
A-scramble for rhyme lest the scan make a muss.
But nowadays, due to the work of a pack 'o
Modernist bards and poetical wackos,
There aren't any rules. You can do what you want.
You don't have to, *e.g.*, end this line with "daunt."
Just to your emotions give long-winded venting,
    And show it's not prose by frequent indenting.
Just one restriction you can't throw out:
Don't give the poem to the girl it's about.

W is for Women. They're awful, mendacious,
Nasty and selfish, cruel and salacious,
As thievish as gypsies, more crazy than Celts.
Be sure that you never fuck anything else.

X is for the attitude of eXistential anomie.
The French mean nothing by it, and neither do we.
So don't go around acting like Jean Paul Belmondo.
Aspire instead to three cars and a condo.

Y is for Your future, supposedly pared
By nuclear-holocaust world-end nightmare.
Don't get disconcerted by apocalyptic jive.
It's been just about to happen since 1945.
And no matter the MIRVs, ICBMs, and SAMs,
It's not going to happen before final exams.

Z is for Zany, eternal class clown,
Who won't stop kidding, who won't sit down.
Bane of the Boys' Dean, cursed by the teachers,
Source of amusement in classrooms and bleachers.
Zany is cute in a kitten or pup.
But as an adult, please shut the fuck up.

Horrible Protestant Hats

〰〰〰〰〰〰〰〰〰〰〰〰〰〰〰〰〰〰〰〰〰〰〰

I was getting ready to go outdoors on a drizzly afternoon. I put on a trench coat, picked up an umbrella, and deposited a waterproof canvas rain hat on my head. My girlfriend, a Catholic, began to laugh and point. "Oh!" she said, "what a horrible Protestant hat!" I looked in the mirror. True, the porkpie-style Brooks Brothers rain hat with the brim turned down on all sides does give one the look of . . . well, a poorly machined something on a recalled American car. It set me thinking.

Protestants *do* wear terrible hats, especially well-off adult male Protestants of the type we usually call WASPs. They wear woven-vegetable-matter summer hats with madras hatbands. These look like hospital gifts that died at the florists. They wear "Irish" tweed hats no self-respecting Irishman would put on his plowhorse. They wear herringbone wool caps that can give a bank president the semblance of a rioting English coalminer. Old artsy WASPs wear embarrassing berets. Middle-aged WASPs who've just gotten a divorce and a sports car wear dopey suede touring caps with a snap on the brim. Then there are the unspeakable hats favored by federal investigative agents and the fur Astrakhans worn by lawyers who, I guess, want their clients to think they run a gulag on the side.

Beyond city limits the situation is worse. Where I live in New England the summer people look like they're trying to prove that slouch hats cause Down's syndrome in adults. Panama hats produce a different effect—imbecility combined with moral turpitude. And there is no polite phrase in English for what a vacationing financial services executive looks like in a Greek fisherman's cap.

Getting anywhere near the water seems to produce WASP hat lunacy. Fly fishermen wear astonishing things on their heads and always decorate them with dozens of dry flies as though at any minute they might dip their very skulls into the torrent and land giant trout with their necks. It's hard to look more stupid than a deep-sea fisherman does in his swordbill cap. Hard, but not impossible. The ordinary Kennebunk cruiser hat accomplishes the task. This is simply the cap from a child's sailor suit with its brim yanked down over eyes, ears, and sometimes nose. Worn thus it resembles nothing so much as a white cotton condom for the brain. Boat hats, indeed, run the gamut of foolery starting with the simple watch cap, making its wearers seem only unlettered, and winding up with the enormous yellow rubber sou'wester foul-weather chapeau, in which even George Bush would look like a drunk cartoon character doing a tuna-fish commercial.

Snow and other frozen forms of water make for no improvement. If there is anything—vassalage, Bolshevism, purdah—more deleterious to the spirit of human dignity than the knit ski cap, I have not seen it. Professional circus clowns, medieval court jesters, Trans-Carpathian village idiots—any one of them would balk at wearing a five-foot-long purple, green, red, pink, and orange cranial sock with a yard-wide pom-pom on the end. And even this is not so bad as what a WASP will wear in the winter when *not* on the ski slopes. That is when he goes out to shovel the walk in a vinyl-brimmed plaid cap with earflaps that tie up over the head—the worst hat on earth, the hat that turned America's Midwest into the world's laughingstock.

I am only half Protestant, but when I look on my closet shelf I find a disgusting Moose River canoeing hat, a regrettable corduroy Cragsmere, an incredibly idiotic Florida Keys bonefishing hat with brims at both ends, several crownless tennis visors that make me look like an Olympic contestant in double-entry bookkeeping, a John Lennon cap left over from my hippie days, and a plethora of the ubiquitous ad-emblazoned baseball caps. To judge by these I have been renting out frontal-lobe space to Purolator, Firestone, the NRA, and the Kittery, Maine, 1978 Jubilee Days. And let's not even discuss the International Signal Orange dunce cap I wear to go bird shooting.

Now, it's true, other ethnic groups also wear unusual headgear. Blacks, Orthodox Jews, Mexican archbishops, Italian steelworkers, to name a few. But the Stetsons of 125th Street are intentionally outrageous, yarmulkes are items of religious faith, and so forth. WASPs wear their hats in all seriousness, without spiritual reasons or historical traditions for doing so, and not a single one of their bizarre toppers would be any help if an I-beam fell on it. Nonetheless a WASP will tell you his hat is functional. It has been my experience that whenever anyone uses the word "functional" he's in the first sentence of a lame excuse. The real reason WASPs wear goofy hats is that goofy-hat wearing satisfies a deep-seated need. *In gin-and-tonic veritas.* Give a WASP six drinks and he'll always put something silly on his head—a lampshade, ladies' underwear, Gorham silver nut dish, L. L. Bean dog bed, you name it. In more sober and inhibited moments he'll make do with an Australian bush hat, a tam-o'-shanter, or the Texan monstrosity all WASPs affect when they get within telexing distance of a cow.

Until the last years of the Eisenhower era, WASPs wore

wonderful haberdashery. They went about in perfectly blocked and creased homburgs, jaunty straw boaters, majestic opera hats, and substantial bowlers. A gentleman would sooner wear two-tone shoes to a diplomatic reception than appear in public without a proper hat. Then something happened.

Adult male Protestants of the better-off kind are a prominent social group. They make up a large percent of our national leaders in business, politics, and education. Maybe it's no accident that the rise of the silly hat coincides with the disappearance of a coherent American foreign policy, the decay of business ethics, the increase in functional illiteracy, and the general decline of the United States as a world power. The head is symbolic of reason, discipline, good sense, and self-mastery. Putting a fuzzy green Tyrolean hat decorated with a tuft of deer behind on top of it means trouble. Our native aristocracy, those among us with the greatest advantages, the best resources, and the broadest opportunities to do good, have decided to abrogate all civilized responsibilities, give free play to the id, and run around acting like a bunch of . . .

Wait a minute! Down by the dock—I just saw a WASP with a pitcher of martinis trying to put a fedora on his dog. Does this mean Henry Kissinger will be made Secretary of State again?

The Ends
of the
Earth

In Search of the
Cocaine Pirates

~~~~~~

I had money in the bank, a pretty girlfriend, an assignment from a slick magazine to interview some business executives. That is, I was bored, restless, and irritable. The difference between journalists and other people is that other people spend their lives running from violence, tragedy, and horror and we spend ours trying to get in on it. Blood was running through the streets of San Salvador, commie choppers thrashed the hills of Afghanistan, Africa was positively in the toilet from Addis Ababa to the Cape, and here I was in a goddam luxury hotel waiting to have lunch with a friendly corporate VP. I longed for stray mortar rounds, typhus epidemics, starving babies at the very least. Please understand, this isn't courage or a desire to tell the world the truth. It's sloth. Nothing makes an easier lead sentence than a stray mortar round hitting a starving baby in a typhus hospital. That is Pulitzer stuff. But try writing even a dependent clause about an honest comptroller giving you net sales figures over pasta salad.

In this funk of self-pity, a headline caught my eye: "Caribbean Islands' Top Officials Held in Drug Smuggling Plot." It seemed that on March 6, 1985, in a Miami Ramada Inn, the Drug Enforcement Agency had arrested Norman Saunders, the chief minister and head of state of a British Crown Colony called the Turks and Caicos Islands. Saunders was videotaped stuffing $20,000 into his pants pockets. He and two other officials from the islands' eleven-member parliament—Minister of Commerce and Development Stafford Missick and legislator Aulden "Smokey" Smith—were charged with seventeen counts of conspiracy to smuggle narcotics. Thus, at day's end, 27 percent of the Turks and Caicos elected government was cooling its heels in a U.S. slammer.

That was more like it. No national magazine had done a story about drug smuggling in the Caribbean for, I don't know, a week. I could fly to the Turks and Caicos in between chats with fiduciary nabobs and get trouble plenty.

Nor was this the first spore of dark narco evil to come whiffing out of these airstrip-dotted, many-harbored cays at the remote southeastern reach of the Bahamas chain. We journalists keep up on such things. For years the English press had been running articles like "Paradise for Pedlars—Island Colony Key to a Multimillion Drug Trade" (*Daily Express,* September 7, 1982). The London *Times* said that in the late seventies "law enforcement officials reckoned that 90 percent[!] of the marijuana entering the United States was being moved through the Turks and Caicos." The *Sunday Telegraph* warned, "Narcotics money is so influential that it is rapidly bringing about the creation of a completely new power structure in the Turks, a whole new political system."

I checked the Saunders story in various newspapers. Apparently the Turks and Caicos natives were not grateful for the DEA's efforts. "Talk of retribution, of hostages . . . and of British warships rushing to the scene" was reported by the *Washington Post* under the front-page headline "Drug Arrests Raise Islands' Tension—

P. J. O'Rourke

~~~~~~

British Governor Urges Populace Not to 'Take to the Streets.' "
The *New York Times* said the new acting chief minister, Mr. Na-
thaniel "Bops" Francis, "declared indignantly that Mr. Saunders
was 'framed' and he spoke angrily of a racist plot hatched by white
Americans." "Aftershocks . . . rumbled through the eight-isle
British territory," read the lead on a *Miami Herald* story which
quoted the commerce minister's nephew as saying, "It's not a
disgrace that they were interested in money. It is a disgrace that
they got caught." And what kind of country has members of Parliament with names like Bops and Smokey, anyway? The place must
be a new pirate republic.

There were a number of these in the Caribbean, Tortuga being
the most famous. It was colonized in the 1600s by a group of
French buccaneers called the Coast Brotherhood. They preyed on
the Spanish plate fleet (and anything else). Another freebooter
mini-nation was New Providence, on the site of modern Nassau.
Founded in 1716, it counted among its citizens "Calico Jack"
Rackham and Edward "Blackbeard" Teach. Rackham was famous
for wearing lightweight cotton clothing, Blackbeard for setting off
firecrackers in his beard and drinking rum and gunpowder. They
robbed ships and killed people too. The head of state in New
Providence was a half-mad castaway the pirates found on the
beach. They styled him "Governor" and made up elaborate official
protocols.

The Turks and Caicos would be up-to-date, of course. There'd
be no Jolly Rogers on the big Herreshoff yachts, just Colombian
registries. Sinister black cigarette speedboats would be bobbing at
the docks, no doubt, Learjets lurking under camouflage nets, big
campesinos in Armani suits fingering their Uzis and MAC-10s while
Guajira Peninsula warlords gestured grandly to scruffy Americans
with Rolex watches. And, naturally, there would be tow-haired,
Hershey-tanned, near-naked dope-dealer girlfriends everywhere—
bodies hard, eyes hard too. Plus bartops slathered with fine-
chopped pink-auraed Andean flake pushed into lines thick as
biceps.

171

Republican Party Reptile

What to pack? Swim suit, flip-flops, .357 magnum . . . On the other hand, given the Latin blow vendors' penchant for murdering wives, infants, not to mention writers, maybe a note from my doctor about taking a sunshine psoriasis cure. The travel brochures made prominent mention of bank secrecy laws, I noticed. The Third Turtle Inn on the island of Providenciales seemed to be the first-rate place to stay. I hit on a cautious, neutral sort of disguise: summer-weight blue blazer, chinos, and deck shoes—a bit lawyer-ish, a touch bankery, just a South Florida yuppie, you know, just brushing shoulders with the scene, in for a little sit-down with a client maybe or bundling some fungibles through a corporate shell. Businesslike, that is, but not *undercover,* for God's sake, or nosy or *too* businesslike. I flew in from Miami. The sweltering tin-roofed airport, the too-casual customs agents, the thornbush-and-palm-scrub landscape all breathed menace. I went to the bar at the Third Turtle, ordered a gin—"Make that a double"—lit a cigarette, and looked knowing.

"Jesus Christ," said somebody in the bar, "another newspaper reporter. How come all you guys wear blue blazers? Is it a *club* or what?"

"Uh," I said. "Er . . . oh . . . I'll bet folks around here are pretty upset about Norman Saunders and everybody getting arrested in Miami," I said, subtly turning the subject toward drugs.

"Upset?!" said someone else, "Goddam right we're upset. Norman and Smokey are the two best tennis players in the islands, and the tournament is *next week!*"

Perhaps this wasn't exactly the story I thought.

The Turks and Caicos rope through eighty miles of ocean. They are outcroppings of eolian limestone, piles of fossil seashell bits, really. There are a few hills, but mostly the islands are near sea level or at it. Mangrove tangles fill the low spots. On first glance, as tropical paradises go, the Ts and Cs are sort of like the roof of your apartment building. Rainfall is scant, topsoil rare. Nice beaches, though, and the wind and water carve the soft rock into rococo shorelines and mysterious sea caves and startling sinkholes fit for Aztec maiden sacrifices. The people are hopelessly friendly. I had to trade in my rented scooter for a Jeep because of so much waving. You don't want to take a hand off the handlebars on what passes for a road down there. A few hundred yards from shore are splendid coral reefs poised on the edge of "the wall," the thousand-meter dropoff at the end of the continental shelf. It's a good place to scuba-dive (or, I mused hopefully, lose a competitor wearing cement Top-Siders). The vegetation is low, harsh, and tangled, but it goes on for miles without human interruption, some of the last truly wild land left in the North Caribbean.

There are thirty-seven islands according to the *New York Times*, forty-two according to the *Washington Post*, eight according to the *Miami Herald*. I counted sixty-three on the only chart I could find, which was also a placemat. Anyone in earshot—taxi drivers, fishing-boat captains, hotel maids, people standing in the road— got involved whenever I asked this question. "East Caicos, West Caicos, North Caicos, South Caicos . . ." Once they started naming islands it was impossible to stop them. ". . . and Middle Caicos and Providenciales and Pine Cay and Grand Turk and Guana Cay and Nigger Cay but we don't call it that anymore and Back Cay and French Cay, Bush Cay, Fish Cays, Big Ambergris, Little Ambergris . . . wait, now, do you mean high tide or low?"

Only eighty-five hundred people live on only six of those islands. Almost as many more are in the Bahamas, Britain, the United States, or somewhere else they can find jobs.

Every spring in the Turks and Caicos there's a hatch of handsome black handspan-sized Erebus moths. They're called "money bats." If they land on you it's said they bring fortune. Obviously they don't bring much. The locals work at conch diving, lobster fishing, a few tourism jobs—there's not a lot to do for a living. In fact, there's not a lot to do.

I interviewed the British governor, the opposition leader, and (the arrested people having politely resigned) the new chief minister and the new minister of commerce, development, and tourism.

Nobody had a bad word, or even an enlightening one, to say

about former chief minister Norman Saunders. He's personable, generous, easy to work with. He's handsome and a tasteful dresser as well. On his home island of South Caicos he commands special affection. His picture is all over the place above a political slogan that sounds like rejected name ideas from "Snow White and the Seven Dwarves": "Firm, Frank, Friendly, Faithful." I was counting on an earful from opposition leader Clement Howell. But they've only had party politics in the Turks and Caicos since 1975, and as yet they seem politely confused about what to do with them. Howell is head of the slightly more populist PDM (Popular Democratic Movement). Saunders was or is head of the slightly more business-oriented PNP (People's National Party). "Sort of like Democrats and Republicans?" I ventured to Howell.

He pondered that. "What's the difference between Democrats and Republicans?"

"The Republicans won."

"Exactly," he said. Was this, I thought, the "whole new political system" the *Sunday Telegraph* had warned about?

Saunders seems to have founded the PNP because another fellow, the late "JAGS" McCartney, had founded the PDM. The PDM was founded because the Turks and Caicos were engaged in what may be history's most halfhearted struggle against British colonialism. This culminated in the "Junkanoo Club incident." In 1975 the British were recruiting Turks and Caicos policemen from other Caribbean islands. JAGS and fellow natives booed the off-island police officers. Some of those officers were, contrary to local custom, wearing guns, and they fired into the air. JAGS and his friends barricaded themselves in the Junkanoo Club and fired into the air back. Hostages were held. Demands were made. (Actually there's some doubt about the hostages. A local newspaper publisher and two other non-PDM characters were in the club, but they were being given unlimited free drinks and may not have known they were hostage.) The principal demand during the Junkanoo Club incident was that a commission be appointed to investigate the Junkanoo Club incident. After an all-night standoff the demand was

P. J. O'Rourke

met. The next year JAGS McCartney was elected the first native chief minister. The struggle for independence ended shortly thereafter when the Thatcher administration told the Turks and Caicos that they were going to be independent whether they liked it or not.

I got ahold of a British Foreign and Commonwealth Office document stamped "RESTRICTED" (though it had been marked down to "Confidential"). This detailed several meetings in London between JAGS and British minister of state Nicholas Ridley. Ridley offered the Turks and Caicos £12 million to become an independent country. JAGS said they wouldn't do it for less than £40 million. Secretary of State Lord Carrington popped in on the conference and "expressed surprise" that the Turks and Caicos were turning down such a generous offer as £12 million "and wondered that the Treasury had agreed to it." JAGS hung tough. The meeting ended on a testy note. "Mr. Ridley . . . offered them a deal, which they could either take or leave. Mr. McCartney said that he would not accept that. Britain was, he said, the captain of the boat and should pay the crew. Mr. Ridley pointed out that we might reduce the crew's wages." JAGS "retorted that in that case, we might have a mutiny. . . . Mr. Ridley made it clear . . . that the problem could be solved by starting again with new people."

In the end the islands got their £12 million and didn't have to be independent either. I asked the British governor what had happened. "It's the post-Falklands era," he sighed.

Anyway, the political system in the Ts and Cs—whether created by narcotics money, crabby twits in the Foreign and Commonwealth Office, or plain old vote-grabbing—is certainly different from ours. Ariel Misick, the minister of commerce, development, and tourism, wanted to talk about commerce, development, and tourism. Imagine a system of governance so unsophisticated that the head of a department knows what his department does. Misick (a distant relation to busted ex-minister Missick-with-two-s's) said there are two hundred square miles of empty Crown Lands in the Turks and Caicos. Two of the largest islands are uninhabited.

Republican Party Reptile

There is half a mile of beach for every hotel room. The Ts and Cs are a last frontier for commercial development in the Caribbean. What about drug-trade fracas and Saunders *et al.?* Well, there had been two people with protest signs on their cars. One of the cars belonged to the contractor who'd built Norman Saunders's new house. It was six months since the last crime of note. "As a lawyer," said Misick, "if I had to depend on going to court to defend people, I'd starve." The only major robbery in Turks and Caicos history was a $600 Cable and Wireless Company payroll heist in 1931.

Governor Christopher J. Turner wanted to talk about development too. Balanced development—nice tourists in big boats, cruising, diving, sport fishing. His other points of hope for the underemployed: the fishing industry, financial services, and agronite mining. (Agronite being a kind of sea dirt useful in making driveways and chemical things. There's lots of it around the place.) Turner was also hipped on some Smithsonian Institution research being done about algae farming. It would be exactly like cattle ranching except underwater with algae instead of hay and with Caribbean king crabs as the cows. At least this is what I have in my notes.

What about drugs? Turner, a career civil servant appointed from London with responsibility for the islands' foreign relations and internal security, said, "Yes." A simple fact of geography. The Turks and Caicos are 600 miles from Colombia, 575 miles from Miami. "We'll always remain an interesting possibility to people engaged in the drug trade." Are the Ts and Cs a hotbed of international dope crime? "No. A refueling option." But, said Turner, "In a British dependent territory things like this aren't supposed to go on." He was the one who'd called in the DEA for a "straightforward double sting operation" which stung his own chief minister. Was Turner shocked? Satisfied? Incredulous? Cheesed off? The governor plays the cards close to his chest. "In the event of his being found guilty it would be a personal tragedy and a tragedy for the islands. Saunders had managerial skills." Any turmoil? Turner said, "I told a reporter, 'There's been no protest, no public demon-

strations, and nobody has taken to the streets.' This was reported as 'British Governor Urges Populace Not to Take to the Streets.' "
Alas, that's what comes of using understatement on the press.

One languid guard in full dress uniform was reading a magazine under a picture of Princess Di in the governor's waiting room. His walkie-talkie crackled with a report of an impending possible rain shower. "Just hang in and hold tight, ten-four," said the guard into his radio.

The high point of my trip to the Turks and Caicos was the interview with Chief Minister "Bops" Francis, or, rather, the time I spent waiting for that interview. There I was, actually "sitting in a dusty colonial outpost waiting to speak to a native official." Breeze whispered through palm fronds above the tin-roofed Government House. Bougainvillea—or something that looked like I've always supposed bougainvillea should—crept along the veranda railings. Etc. One doesn't get much of this in a modern journalism career. Next I wanted to go to the "Colonial Club," except there wasn't one, and have a "stingah," whatever that is.

Bops turned out to be a nice old man who was sick of talking to reporters. "I've commented all I can." He was miffed at the way the DEA had treated Saunders, the head of a sovereign or semisovereign or something state. "Mr. Saunders," said the chief minister, "is bitter that he was not taken into custody but to a penthouse and kept there waiting for the press to come around." I checked with a *Miami Herald* reporter and this was true. The DEA called newspapers and television stations, held Saunders, Missick, and Smith at the Ramada until media got there, and then marched them, in handcuffs, to a paddy wagon. "I don't think they would do this to a dignitary of the Caucasian race," said Francis. Was Saunders framed? "I've heard it. I believe it." He pointed out that the Turks and Caicos had failed to join the Reagan-sponsored Caribbean Basin Initiative.

"Please do not carry the tone that I condone any actions in drugs," said the chief. "Under my administration there will not be forwarding of any part of the drug trade."

And that was the extent of "Drug Arrests Raise Islands' Tension." I did not see any drugs. I did not smell so much as the faintest bouquet of a burning spliff. The girls all had both ends of their bathing suits on. I met a stern and dangerous-looking Jamaican colonel, but he was working for a UN agency planning hurrican-disaster relief. Nobody, not the police, not the governor's honor guard, carried a gun. A hotel manager in Grand Turk told me there had been "threats of violence." Threats of violence? "Well, over the telephone." I pressed him. "There's a rumor the governor received two crank calls." A taxi driver talked of drug smuggling: "No. I have my children to live for. I have my grandchildren to live for. I want to make my dollar every day and go and enjoy my happy home." A bartender said of his fellow citizens: "People will stick by you if you did right. But if you did wrong I pity you."

The only horror I encountered was flying the local airline. They have a little twin-prop plane. The cowling was off and a dozen mechanics were scampering around the engine. They looked to be sixteen and were working in rhythm to a portable radio. The engine caught fire. One of them ran up from somewhere with a coffee can full of water and splashed it at the burning gasoline. Then they put the cowl back on and we boarded the plane and took off. The thornbush-and-palm-scrub landscape really *did* breathe menace that time, let me tell you.

The Turks and Caicos don't even have a romantic history, maybe the only place in the Caribbean without one. A recent theory does have it that Columbus made his New World landfall on Grand Turk rather than Watlings Island in the Bahamas. But, as Turks and Caicos historian H. E. Sadler puts it, "After a weekend rest, Columbus was anxious to reach China." There's a note in Columbus's log to the effect that some natives he'd taken prisoner "signed to me that there were very many islands, so many that they could not be counted, and they mentioned by their name more than a hundred"—apparently a local pastime since at least 1492.

The Turks got their name from the French slang for "pirate," but actual pirate activity there was desultory. Calico Jack Rackham did operate out of North Caicos after the Brits cleaned house in New Providence. But Jack was not much as a swashbuckler. His crews twice mutinied on him because of his cowardice. He was most notable for his girlfriend Anne Bonny, a foul-mouthed vixen who dressed as a man, wore a brace of pistols, and wielded a serious cutlass in the hand-to-hand stuff. Bonny had a roving eye. She got a crush on a handsome young sailor in Rackham's crew, made a pass, and discovered the sailor was one Mary Reid, also dressed as a man. The two became best friends. When Rackham was finally cornered by the British navy, he surrendered while Anne and Mary battled on to the last and then escaped death sentences by getting pregnant. As Calico Jack stood on the gallows, Anne Bonny said to him, "If you had fought like a man you would not now be about to hang like a dog." They were quite a bunch. But they didn't really spend much time in the Ts and Cs.

Other notable events in the Turks and Caicos annals:

- 1783—Admiral Horatio Nelson failed to recapture Turks and Caicos from the French. (In one of his less heroic dispatches Nelson stated, "With such a force and their strong situation, I did not think anything farther could be attempted.") Later the French gave the islands back anyway.
- 1788—Forty Tory families fled the American Revolution, bringing twelve hundred slaves with them. They tried to grow cotton, failed, and split, leaving the slaves to fend for themselves.
- 1962—John Glenn splashed down near Grand Turk.
- 1966—Queen Elizabeth visited. A donkey race was held in her honor.

I did a lot of hard drinking, some deep-sea fishing, more hard drinking, much hanging out on the beach, some drinking in the daytime—all for the sake of research, mind you. And I came up with a few drug-smuggling anecdotes like the one about the South Caicos businessman who had been, I suppose, sampling his own wares and walked into the propeller of his airplane. Umptity kilos of powdered self-esteem were left sitting on the tarmac and nobody on the island slept for a month. Another smuggler, on Providenciales, tried to bring his plane in from Miami at night. There are no lights at the Provo airport, so he phoned his wife and told her to take the pickup truck, drive down to the end of the strip, and turn on the high beams. He landed on top of her. This incident didn't exactly have anything to do with drugs. The smuggler had been in Miami to go grocery shopping. But anyway, wife and smuggler survived, though airplane and pickup were a mess.

In 1980 the DEA launched Operation Bat, designed to intercept and disrupt boat-borne marijuana shipments. An Air Force C5A cargo plane landed unannounced at Provo, scaring the hell out of everyone. The C5A was filled with speedboats. Ten DEA agents carrying automatic weapons pitched tents in all the places with the worst mosquitoes. Within a week every speedboat had been run aground and smashed on the countless (though not nameless) cays and sandbars.

Then there was the plane full of bootleg Quaaludes which made a fuel stop at South Caicos on its way from South America to the States. But the pilot didn't have any cash on him. He had to leave his drug shipment as security for the gasoline. The airport employees gave the pills away. People in the Turks and Caicos had never seen a Quaalude. They'd take them three or four at a time. There was a spate of eccentric driving. Cars were smashed in trees, cars were up on porches, cars were out in the ocean all over the islands. A week later the pilot came back with the money. No 'ludes. He was pissed. He came back again a few days later with three hombres carrying M-16s. One customs agent was at the airport when they landed. He ran off down the road howling in fear. The hombres and pilot were ready for vengeance, but there was no way to get anywhere to find anyone to wreak the vengeance on. An old Volkswagen was parked at the airport, key in the ignition. But it wouldn't start. They stood around for a while, then gave up and flew away.

P. J. O'Rourke

In the matter at hand—the United States of America vs. Norman Saunders, Stafford Missick, and Alden Smith a/k/a Smokey—there's also basis in some genuine hanky-panky. Saunders owns the fuel concession at that South Caicos airport. He did a lot of night business. And Saunders was living better than he should have been on his $18,816 chief minister's salary and the profits from an airplane gas station on a landing strip with one scheduled flight a day. He had a fair-sized house built on Grand Turk, a kind of Samoan-style peaked-roof affair looking like the Trader Vic family mausoleum. Local gossip says it cost $1.2 million, an estimate that's surely high and outside. But it is on the beach two doors from the governor's mansion. Saunders has a big car and a yacht. At election time there was a scad of campaign money bouncing and fluttering around in his South Caicos parliamentary district. Missick, too, has a nice house and an Oldsmobile. I don't know about Smokey. Generally speaking, there are more items of gold jewelry, Piaget watches, and Michael Jackson fashion jackets on the local population than you'd expect in a place where the last time anybody painted a building was 1956.

But it was ever thus all through the seedy archipelagos of the Caribbean. There never has been an unnaughty way to make a living. In the Turks and Caicos the traditional livelihood was raking up evaporated sea salt—an industry in gradual decline since 1780. In 1964 it petered out completely, leaving smelly pools of half-evaporated brine all over the islands. Other than that the only profession was salvaging the thousands of neighboring shipwrecks —most caused, probably, by distracted harbor pilots using placemats to navigate and trying to get the natives to shut up about what all the islands are called. Sometimes the locals would get overenterprising. In 1864 an American frigate ran aground off North Caicos "and the Captain was forced to retire to his quarter deck and prevent the incursion of Salvagers with force of arms." All through the nineteenth century there were complaints of false lights being set out to drum up business. I like to think the smuggler's wife in the pickup truck was an unintentional party to this old tradition.

181

Some islanders, mainly white ones, will tell you that it was Saunders's predecessor, JAGS McCartney, who was involved in the drug trade and that when Saunders and the PNP came in the smugglers seemed to disappear. Certainly JAGS, who sported mild dreadlocks, looked a bit more criminal. When he and his cohorts were elected, they all flew to Haiti and had identical leisure suits made. If you fired anybody in the PDM, they'd come over to your house, all dressed alike, and glower. But JAGS is revered today, and the PDM supporters I met were the most likable people in the islands. Plus the present PDM leader, Clement Howell, has a reputation for probity standing somewhere between Lincoln's and Mom's. Yet JAGS died in a suspicious plane crash while flying to Atlantic City with a reputed American crime figure. However, it was also JAGS who first appealed to the British government for help in combating drug traffic. Who knows? There are no facts south of Palm Beach.

Saunders, if he was doing anything, was doing nothing that didn't come naturally; 250 years ago Governor Bruere of Bermuda complained, "The Caicos trade did not fail to make its devotees somewhat ferocious." And one official replied, "Sir—you'll have business enough upon your hands if you go about to rectify that, for there is not a man that sails from hence, but will trade with a pirate." Especially if he's offered a deal like the one the DEA was offering Saunders. The DEA, by its own admission, had undercover agents promise Norman Saunders $250,000 a week to refuel drug planes. We had an interesting discussion one night in the bar of the Third Turtle Inn. Everyone—foursquare businessmen on fishing vacations, fat American tourists, the kitchen help, me, honeymoon couples—I mean every *one* of us said we'd refuel dope planes for $250,000 a week. What *wouldn't* we do for $250,000? After a certain number of drinks some pretty frightening admissions were heard.

Later I would go back to Miami and root through complaints, indictments, affidavits, and so forth. In a sworn deposition, a DEA special agent with the unprepossessing name of Gary Sloboda said . . . well, he said all sorts of things. The document rambles on for sixteen pages, chronicling what amounts to a lot of big talk. No presence of an actual drug is mentioned anywhere. And every person who talked to Saunders about dope was some kind of DEA agent, informant, or plant except one loudmouth French Canadian named André who stumbled into these bull sessions and began announcing what a scam artist he was. Despite the palaver about astronomy-sized payoffs, it seems Saunders was given only sixty grand and ten of that was to pay off a fuel bill run up by an informant's business partner. Smokey got $2,500.

The hard evidence presented to the grand jury was yet less magisterial. Various meetings were secretly tape-recorded. Here's a sample page from the transcript:

SMOKEY—Let's say, lets say it was about two thousand just for them at the airport

CONFIDENTIAL INFORMANT: Huh

SMOKEY—(Unintelligible)

C.I.—How do you know?

SMOKEY—(Unintel.)

C.I.—One of those black haired

SMOKEY—(Unintel.)

C.I.—I don't know a fucking thing about

SMOKEY—(Unintel.)

SAUNDERS—(Unintel.)

SAUNDERS—Let's say OK look at some figures. Lets say we're talking about two thousand each, that's just throwing out some numbers (Unintel.) If you give two guys in the tower four thousand, two times four is eight thousand, and (unintel.)

SMOKEY—Alright fuck em.

Republican Party Reptile

I watched the videotape where Saunders stuffs $20,000 into his pants pockets. I mean, the man's not at the Ramada for his health. Somebody does say, "Here's twenty thousand," and he does stuff it into his pants pockets. Other than that it was hard to tell what was going on. The tape was shot with a pinhole lens stuck through a wall at the level of an electrical outlet. What I saw was mostly knees and behinds. The drug agent and the drug informant talked about drugs. The ratchet-jawed Canuck kept putting his two cents in. The DEA guys reiterated everything they said, obviously for the benefit of a hidden microphone. The only words from Norman Saunders that I could make out were: "We're talking about fees. A sort of finder's fee." As of this writing Saunders is finding himself in prison, bail set at $1.1 million.

It seems to me the Drug Enforcement Agency picked the Turks and Caicos as a nice lackadaisical place, a place with a friendly NATO-ally administration, a place that was an easy target. No stonewalling commies or angry armed peasants or touchy black-power governments here. Governor Turner said the very reason the Turks and Caicos are popular with drug smugglers is that the people are law-abiding. "There's no violence, no rip-offs, no shake-downs."

And they are lovely islands. And the Third Turtle really is first-rate—excellent food, big, airy rooms opening onto terraces above the beach, great bar. And the expanse of wilderness is wonderful. There's no clog of high-rise condos or clots of dippy shops and prissy restaurants, just miles of verdant land aroil with bird and lizard life where perhaps no human has stood since hungry Carib Indian invaders chased edible Arawak natives into the brush.

On Providenciales I took my Jeep an hour's trip out a near-impassable track to eight miles of untouched beach and cliffs. I found a little cove between two great rocks where the waves came up on Clairol sand. I took my clothes off and all morning disported myself like Brooke Shields in *Blue Lagoon* (about as much chest but more stomach).

P. J. O'Rourke

~~~~~~

Back at the Third Turtle I was writing in my notebook—
"Drugs—can't find any"; "Pirates—a lot of hooey"—when I heard
the unmistakable bellow of the redneck Gulf Coast man of affairs,
the peckerwood entrepreneur, the Snopes with an M.B.A. "Two
hundert square miles of un-de-veloped beachfront . . . God *damn!*
I *tell* you what we gotta do! You know that Golden Door place?
Where the fat ladies go? How about wunna them! And how about
with a goddam *cosmetic surgery* clinic right attached? Huh? How
'bout *that!?* God *damn!!!*" Ah. Well. I crossed out "a lot of hooey."

With Hostage and Hijacker in Sunny Beirut

~~~~~~

Boarding Middle East Airlines flight 804 from London to Lebanon, I was picking out the terrorist. The guy in the shiny suit who looked like Danny Thomas—it wasn't him. The exhausted mother with three children under three—it wasn't her. Then dozens of swarthy youths, bearded to the eyes, came trotting on board. They wore the off-brand blue jeans and pilled-up synthetic polo shirts that are the usual mufti of the Lebanese militias. "Allah akbar!" they shouted as the plane took off, which just means "God is great" but always sends a chill up my backside. As the hoot of the Moslem fundamentalist, it carries a meaning like "Jesus loves you!" would if Jerry Falwell and his friends were running around America murdering Episcopalians. I headed for the toilet to take a nervous leak and size up my flying companions. There was one bunch standing by the galley. I leaned in close to see who had the fragmentation grenade in his duty-free shopping bag. "Yalluh!" They jumped back in alarm. "Awk!" I did too. "CIA!!" said their horrified faces. What a letdown. With blue eyes and striped necktie, the most suspicious-looking person on the airplane was me.

I don't know why any of us was getting in a sweat. The only way to *keep* from being hijacked to Beirut these days is to buy a commercial ticket and fly there.

Beirut International Airport was a *Weekly Reader* current-events quiz made manifest. Here was the Amal in force. There was a blown-up Royal Jordanian passenger plane. And right at our wingtip was the pirated TWA jet. Somewhere off in the snakes-and-ladders maze of the Shiite neighborhoods, thirty-six American tourists were in a pickle. The whole scene set me to thinking about the villainy of human motivation, mostly my own. I mean, I was delighted for the excuse to be back in Lebanon. I like to hang around places where human nature is at its most baffling.

Lebanon sits on the thin neck of the Fertile Crescent, an arable strip no more than forty miles wide that joins the great basins of Mesopotamia and the Nile. From this flinder of sparsely watered top spoil come our alphabet, our religion, and, in the form of the first agriculture, our civilization itself. Who holds "The Mountain," as the Lebanese call it, stands athwart the trade routes of Africa and Asia, controls the eastern Mediterranean, and has a grip on the remote-control garage-door opener to Europe or something like that. No fan of social chaos can help but thrill to tread ground fought over by Canaanites, Egyptians, Assyrians, Babylonians, Persians, Greeks, Romans, Arabs, Turks, French, British, more Arabs, and occasional U.S. Marines. It's been a five-thousand-year tag-team match, and, what's more, the crazy oafs are still in the ring. Philistines, Nazarenes, Israelites, peoples of the great Syrian desert, and strange *firinghi* European interlopers are, to this very day, tossing half nelsons on each other and flailing away with rabbit punches and illegal flying dropkicks.

A friend had sent one of Lebanon's innumerable "fixers" to meet me at the airport. "Mr. Bisgee! Mr. Bisgee!" ("P.J." is quite beyond the Arab tongue.) This sweaty, amiable little man shoved me in front of fifty people at passport control, dragooned a porter, fended off a bribery touch from a Lebanese army officer, whisked me uninspected through customs, and put me in a chauffeured car. The Lebanese understand trouble. That is, they understand the only understandable thing about it. There's always a buck to be made when trouble's afoot.

Six months ago nearly all American newsmen were pulled out of Lebanon. Terrorism was one reason, but so was the lack of a "hometown hook." The only other Americans left in the country were seven obscure kidnap victims and some embassy duffs. Neither group lent itself to vibrant coverage. So what if man's fate might depend on the ugly events hereabouts? Stateside coverage dwindled to a few paragraphs in the international "Deaths Elsewhere" column. Now, however, *Hostages II* was playing, and scribblers, Nikon hounds, tape jockeys, and talking heads were in from the ends of the earth. The Lebanese middlemen couldn't have been happier if the Marines had invaded, and they might just yet.

I checked into the Summerland Hotel on the seafront in Beirut's south suburbs. The Summerland is a great three-sided, four-tiered resort complex with shopping center, health club, sauna, restaurants, and a beauty salon. In the Summerland's center court are three swimming pools, a spiral water slide, an artificial grotto with waterfall, a small-boat harbor, and a private beach. Two acres of deck chairs were covered with tan bodies. The smooth Arab girls wearing makeup poolside looked to have been teleported from a Westchester country club.

This doesn't match your mental picture of Beirut. But Beirut doesn't match any mental picture of anything. After ten years of polygonal civil war and invasions and air strikes by Syrians, Israelis, and multilateral peace-keeping forces, the place still isn't as squalid as some cities that have never been hit by anything but government social programs. There are zones of manic destruction, of course. The Green Line looks like an antinuke-benefit-concert album cover. The Bois de Pins, planted in the 1600s, has taken so many rocket attacks that it's a forest of phone poles. Hotel Row along the Corniche was destroyed in the first year of warfare. The best hotel, the St. George, is a burned hulk. But its bar is still open and people water-ski from the beach there in all but the worst of the fighting. "What about snipers?" I once asked someone. He said, "Oh, most of the snipers have automatic weapons. They aren't very accurate."

Everywhere there are chips and chucks out of buildings and buildings missing entirely, but there are also cranes and construction gangs and masons and plasterers. Maybe nowhere else has a city been built and destroyed at the same time. Electricity is intermittent and the garbage hasn't been collected since the late 1970s, but the shops are full of all the world's imports. And with no trade quotas or import duties or government to enforce them if they existed, goods are cheap. Not an hour passes without gunfire or explosion, but the traffic jams are filled with Mercedes sedans.

The Summerland itself sits bracketed by the bombed ruins of another resort and by a principal Amal checkpoint. At the checkpoint the wrong kind of beachgoer can be pulled out of his car and taken away and shot. Beirut is a sort of Janus-faced monument to the entire history of man. He will endure, but what a shithead.

Anyway, drugs are cheap, about $50 a gram for cocaine. Some friends and I sniffed piles of it and emptied the minibars in two hotel rooms. About midnight it seemed like a good idea to go out. Street fighting had been desultory. We could probably make it to a nightclub.

ABC News had its headquarters at the Summerland. We stopped to say hello. It was "day 15," as they say in hostage crises, and everybody was settling in. We all figured the thing would be good for at least a month, maybe three. We stood around yammering wisely about Arab intransigence and how time has no meaning in the East. Then somebody, I think it was Chris Harper, ABC's Rome bureau chief, stepped out onto a balcony and stepped right back in looking like he'd caught the family dog playing the cello. Directly below us on the wide flagstone terrace by the double-

Republican Party Reptile

Olympic-size pool were thirty-two American hostages. The Amal had brought them to the Summerland for dinner.

Let me tell you, they looked terrible. I don't mean they looked abused. They just looked like American tourists do everywhere—elastic-waisted loaf-around slacks, T-shirts with dim slogans and embarrassing place names, waffle-soled sandals worn with socks. These people had been thrust into a dramatic situation with vast international implications and, frankly, they weren't dressed for it.

I think history deserves at least rumpled linen suits and sweat-stained panama hats. And what's a possible world war without something to drink? But Amal is very opposed to that sort of thing. Instead everybody stood around for about two hours munching snacks and sipping fruit juice while waiters got a giant banquet table ready.

It was a Rotary Club men's breakfast in the middle of the night at Club Med with guns—sort of. The hostages looked confused. The more so since some reporters knew some Amal guards and were chatting them up. You could hear tourist minds clicking over—"Oh, God, they're *all* in it together." Which, in a sense, is true, but it's the kind of insight that makes for really tedious *New York Times* op-ed-page pieces on the role of the media.

The captive dinner guests, poor devils, were a bit wooden and formal at first. They had the eggshell walk and stiff solemn movements that come from long-accumulated fear. At least everyone on the terrace knew how they felt. You can't spend time in this part of the earth and not be familiar with the indissoluble cold softball beneath the diaphragm, the slow hyperventilation, the runny feeling in the bowels and wet flesh creepiness along the limbs. It sucks.

Maybe for this reason everybody behaved himself. There was no blast of camera lights or lewd thrust of microphones from the reporters. The hostages didn't whimper for mercy or ask the President to A-bomb us all. The Amal guards were casual, propping their guns against the stone planters and gathering in little groups to smoke cigarettes. They let their charges wander around the courtyard unescorted and amble down to the beach.

P. J. O'Rourke

ABC had three telephone lines held permanently open to the United States, and the engineers wired one into a poolside phone so everybody could call his folks.

I wish I could say it was fascinating. One hostage began giving me a complete inside story of what had gone on since they'd been removed from the plane. I was scribbling madly on a napkin. "You've all been in communication with each other, then?" I said. "No," said the hostage, "I heard this on BBC World News."

Ridley Moon said he wanted a stiff drink. Victor Amburgy had had dysentery and had lost so much weight he was falling out of his pants. Kurt Carlson told me his younger brother, Bun, is the drummer for Cheap Trick. Jack McCarty said he and some of the others had been working up notes for a *Hostage Handbook*. "Bring Toilet Paper" was one chapter heading. A little forehead-sized pillow is another good idea, he said, and told me how at one point when they were still on the plane they'd been forced to keep their heads between their knees for six hours. "I'd stopped smoking before this happened," said Kurt Carlson. Great events are something like doughnuts for all that's right at the center of them.

And so the reluctant houseguests went home with their hosts, though not before an Amal guard brought one guy back because he hadn't had a chance to phone home. Could we—journalists and hostages together—have overpowered the slack and outnumbered Amal guards? Could we have mounted fire from the Summerland's ramparts, phoned the Sixth Fleet and held out until rescue choppers arrived? It would be a marketable movie premise. Nothing like real guns to show how lousy popular art is.

I got into bed at 4:00 that morning with an uneasy mind. There are supposed to be U.S. spy satellites that can read the headlines on newspapers. I know there are radio listening posts all over the Middle East, and the Amal guys were on their walkie-talkies all night. Every would-be Jimmy Carter antonym on the National Security Council must have heard about the dinner at the Summerland by now. It would be just like U.S. foreign policy to send Delta Force in an hour late. I could see it all—concussion bombs in the swimming pools, Hueys tangled in the beach umbrellas, and hyperadrenalinized Marine sergeants indiscriminately rescuing the wrong people from a bunch of sleepy room-service waiters. I left the door to my balcony open. If I was going to be dragged to safety and someplace American Express could find me, the last thing I wanted was a six-by-four-foot broken glass slider added to my hotel bill.

At the end of the Friday-night dinner the Summerland Hotel staff had brought out a huge cake with chocolate lettering across the top: "Wishing you all a happy trip back home." Saturday morning the U.S. State Department announced the hostages' release. So did the Syrian government. Various networks and wire services carried the story. It seemed like a lot of people were getting their news from cake frosting.

In fact, nobody had gone much of anywhere. The thirty-two dinner hostages and the plane crew had been gathered in a school in a Shiite slum, the Burj Barajna. But the extraradical Hizbullah Shiites were refusing to cough up the four extra hostages they had stashed in a basement somewhere.

Hizbullah wouldn't release the other four because . . . well, you have to understand Lebanese politics. It's sort of like a gang war because the militias are organized in normal Mediterranean friends-of-Frank-Sinatra style and control the drug traffic and smuggling. It's sort of like a real war because Syria, Israel, the PLO, etc. are irked at each other and commit most of their irksomeness on Lebanese territory. It's sort of like a race riot because every religious group thinks it's being treated like niggers and thinks every other group should be. And it's sort of like an American presidential election because most of the worst things in life are. It's insane. It's incomprehensible. Everybody in the place ought to be whacked over the head. The whole business is almost as horrid as New York City during rush hour. (Though not, I think, as horrid as New York would be if our national system of checks and balances called in sick and Syria, Israel, Russia, the United States,

Iran, and North Korea gave everybody who could make a flag free guns and a dump truck full of money.)

Beats me. I went out to the airport and watched hot, grumpy photographers on stakeout at the TWA jet. I stood on top of the control tower and got something—a pistol, a finger, a rolled-up copy of the TWA in-flight magazine—pointed at me from the cockpit window. There were a lot of reporters and TV producers talking into paper bags. This is because the militiamen call you a spy if you have a two-way radio, and also because the militiamen love two-way radios and calling you a spy at gunpoint is a good way to get a free one.

Nothing happening here. I went back to the Summerland and poked around in the ABC office. A newsroom had been created by hauling the beds out of five hotel rooms and shipping in 2,500 kilos of electronic gear. There were three bureau chiefs in the place, and correspondents, producers, editors, technicians, camera crews, drivers, and money men all yelling orders at each other while the open phone lines disgorged useful suggestions from the ABC brass in New York:

"Hello, Beirut. We have a report from the Muncie, Indiana, *Advertiser-Wasp* that the hostages have been moved to Senegal. Would you confirm?"

"Hello, Beirut. Is Kahlil Gibran still alive? Could we get him on the wire for a *Good Morning America* phoner?"

"Hello, Beirut. Radio New Zealand says five of the hostages have mumps."

I'm used to the quiet life of free-lance writers where we just go home and make things up. This looked more like the time my little sister knocked my ant farm off the dresser.

I sat down in one of the five hotel rooms and watched the tapes ABC was sending out, like I'd watch pay TV in any hotel room except with a mess of old coffee cups, wine bottles, room-service trays, and cigarette butts even worse than the one I usually accumulate. There was gunfire on the screen, gunfire outside too. Weird. Reminded me of those sixties acid wallows where, you know, like *this* is the movie and you're watching it, but, like, you're *in* it and . . . The medium is the message, indeed.

Darn good coverage, though, I thought: swell get-a-load-of-this-guy smile from Captain Testlake with that gun-waving Hizbullah bunny behind him, nice earnest hostage interviews (one guy told his wife to pay the mortgage, though I don't think that got on the air), and deeply important (if slightly dull-o) talks with Nabih Berri (who doesn't speak English worse than most people who've lived in Detroit).

I understand that back home there was a lot of argle-bargle about what the networks were doing during *America Held Hostage: The Sequel.* But you have to remember a television has two sides. I was up by the head. What came out the other end, I can't tell you. For all I know *Eyewitness News* starred Donny and Marie and featured commentary by Koko, the gorilla who uses computers to talk.

That night a young man named Jaafar Jalabi arrived at the ABC office. He was a friend of Nabih Berri and had been sent over to explain the real reason that the hostages hadn't been released. I liked him immediately. For one thing he was scared, and there's entirely too much bravery in Lebanon. Also he wore a Rolex. I have a personal theory that faithful, disciplined, highly principled, self-sacrificing people (in other words the people who are forever getting the rest of us killed) wear cheap wristwatches.

Hizbullah, said Jaafar, was refusing to release its Americans because President Reagan had said in a speech, "I don't think anything that attempts to get people back who've been kidnapped by thugs, murderers, and barbarians is wrong to do." Who knows how Hizbullah threaded its way through the syntax in that statement. Jaafar admitted any excuse probably would have done. A bureau chief led him off to make everything clear to Peter Jennings and the American public.

When Jaafar was through I asked him how he'd gotten dragged into this. He said Berri knew he'd gone to college in the United States and therefore it was felt he understood America. (So much for the theory of "highly sophisticated Shiite manipulation of American public opinion." The last time a U.S. college student understood America, they shot him at Kent State.) "What's going to happen," I asked, "when the hostage crisis is over? Are the various Shiite factions going to . . . you know . . . ?"

"I've got a speedboat anchored down there," said Jaafar, looking toward the Summerland's little harbor, "and it's packed with food and supplies." That was something to remember. No matter how interested you are in social chaos, it's always a good idea to keep an eye on the emergency exit.

Sunday morning I went down to the school in the Burj Barajna. The Amal said this time for sure they were getting all the loose Americans rounded up and out of there. The ride over was a lesson in what a rescue mission would have required. My Lebanese driver couldn't find the place with a map. I suppose Delta Force could have stopped and asked directions like we did, but the Lebanese can be long-winded that way. My guess is our strike force would still be drinking tiny cups of coffee and trying to get out of buying a rug and a case of smuggled Marlboros.

The Burj was not really a slum, just an old neighborhood with haphazard alleys for streets and five-story stucco apartment buildings with gardens walled by breeze block. Dozens of these neighborhoods have been destroyed in the civil war, and creeping Miami Beachism was destroying them anyway before the war began. Small girls in what looked like first-communion dresses giggled in the doorways. Small boys followed the militiamen around and inspected the press corps' equipment. Moms, dads, and quite a lot of attractive teenage daughters were standing on the balconies and looking out the windows with the usual tenement dwellers' interest in local brouhaha. There were no chadors in evidence and not as many scarves as you'd see on the British royal family at the average horse show. This, then, is your howling mob of fanatical Shiites praying for martyrdom and dripping blood from the fangs.

The reporters were an uglier bunch by far. There were a

hundred or more of them ganged up in the alley by the school. They looked as bad as the hostage tourists but fatter and meaner and dressed in even more ridiculous tropical travel clothes. With their panoply of tote bags, cameras, carryalls, haversacks, and phrase books, they seemed a kind of race of supertourists come to avenge the incarceration of their fellows. Indeed, it's been suggested for years that the Beirut media should form their own militia. God knows, there are enough of them. And it would simplify many news stories: "Tonight on *Nightline* Ted Koppel threatens suicide attack unless he meets own demands to free self!"

The Amal were wearing any old thing. Some had on Miller Lite T-shirts and designer Levi's, others were so laden with Kalashnikovs, rocket-propelled grenade launchers, sheath knives, pistols, spare clips, and ammo belts that they could hardly move. They looked like kids playing army. Which is what they are. The average age can't be eighteen. They're violently opposed to the imperialist, Zionist policies of the United States and will, however, if they speak any English, babble about which career they'll pursue in America as soon as they get a Green Card. They have better manners than I ever did as an adolescent. I suspect it's because they're getting to live out all those *Mad Max* fantasies in their own backyards.

I committed a breach of Shiite etiquette by kissing Jane Evans, a CNN camerawoman I hadn't seen in six months. One of the Amal kids admonished me with a smile. "You two, you are get married, huh?"

"Yes, yes, of course," I said.

"And have many children?"

Naturally they like to try their weapons. When the press got obstreperous because Amal wouldn't let anyone into the school, the kids cut loose with a dozen rounds of AK-47 fire. Your stomach muscles contract, you go into a crouch, chemical zaniness spurts through the bloodstream no matter how many times you've heard close fire and no matter that you know the guns are pointed in the air. It's funny, too, seeing a hundred sweaty, red-faced newsmen in silly golf clothes duck-walking backward at sixty miles an hour.

I can't tell you much about how it all ended. The next time you think to ask somebody about something "because he was there," think again. I was there. Some towel-head from Hizbullah marched up and down the street twice. There was a certain amount of what passes for horseplay in these latitudes. "I blow you camera away," said one of the older Amal guys to a network crew. He aimed his pistol. He pulled the trigger. Click. It wasn't loaded. "Ha ha ha ha ha." There was a lot of standing around in the sun with no beer.

About 5:00 in the evening the Amal let a few crews and reporters into the school. "We take one of each kind of type," said a spokesman. "All English-speaking print media!" shouted my friend Robert Fisk from the London *Times,* the bastard. The lucky few got to stand around in the school for another couple hours while Hizbullah dignitaries gave free souvenir Korans to the hostages.

A convoy was standing ready behind Amal lines. I hustled for position so I could witness the send-off. But there are about seven ways out of the Burj and I picked the wrong one. The convoy went down another street and I was left watching a gaggle of French photographers bribe their way onto a balcony that overlooked nothing but more French photographers.

I felt rather forlorn. Here we were, the center of international attention, steeped in high drama, with danger on every side, and enormous expense accounts. Could we face the truth that lies in the dark corners of the heart . . . and admit we were having a really good time? No use, I supposed, asking the hostages to volunteer and stay for a while.

Moving to New
Hampshire

~~~~~~

Not long ago I moved from New York City to a small town in New Hampshire. I didn't know much about country life, but I was in love with New England scenery. I wanted to do my writing in an atmosphere of pastoral serenity. And I felt a need for a healthier life. Also, I'd never had a roof repaired so I thought New York was the most expensive place on earth to live. Since many other city people are moving into the countryside, I feel an obligation to pass along what I've learned. I also feel an obligation to pay for my new roof.

When moving to rural New England, the first consideration is choice of a town. There are three kinds of towns in New England: towns that know they're cute, towns that don't know they're cute, and towns determined to become cute no matter what.

Towns that know they're cute are characterized by high real-estate prices, frequent arts-and-crafts fairs, and numerous Volvos with "Save the Whales" bumper stickers. It's Vermont, really, that specializes in this kind of town. You don't want to live in one of these. The "shoppe" signs are all misspelled, the arts-and-crafts fairs tie up traffic, and (it hurts to tell this to the people in the Volvos) Vermont doesn't *have* any whales.

Towns that don't know they're cute are even worse. Most seem to have zoning regulations requiring lawn ornaments and house trailers in every yard. You'll buy a beautiful home on Main Street and wake up the next morning to find someone else has bought the beautiful home directly across from you, torn it down, and built a gas station. And the teenage natives use the Meeting House's 1690 weather vane for rifle practice. This is painful to those of us with finer aesthetic sensibilities who'd like to make it into a lamp.

The right kind of town is the one determined to become cute. My own town, Jaffrey, is one of these. We're taking up a collection to repair the weather vane, and there's an effort under way to have our Main Street gas station spell Shell with an extra "e." Towns like Jaffrey have civic pride and local spirit, but they have their drawbacks too. Civic pride means committees. And there's always the danger of getting drafted. Last year we had an infestation of gypsy moths. My committee spent three weeks cutting oak leaves out of yellow construction paper and gluing them to tree limbs so sightseers wouldn't be disappointed during the autumn foliage season.

Once you've chosen a town, the next step is to choose a house. There is a general rule about houses in New England: the worse the architecture, the more authentically Colonial the house. If a house has a grand appearance, handsome layout, and large airy rooms, it's Victorian junk. But if you can't, at first glance, tell it from a mobile home, it was built before 1700. Of course, it isn't fair to say that. Very few mobile homes have five-foot ceilings, basements full of water, or sill rot. Anyway, when checking for authenticity, make sure the rooms are the size of bath mats and that the electrical system looks horrid. Our colonial forebears seem to have been notably poor electricians.

One thing you will not have to worry about is your view. Every authentic Colonial house in New England has a splendid view. Just ask the real-estate agent. "View?" said mine. "Of course there's a view! Climb out this window onto the porch roof, Mr. O'Rourke, and shinny up that chimney—absolutely breathtaking."

Actually buying the house will be no different from buying a house anywhere else, except for the title search. New England deed records go back 350 years, and in every one of those years somebody made a mistake. This results in unusual deeds. One property I looked at had fifteen acres. Two acres were in front of the house and the remaining land ran in a three-inch-wide strip fifty-five miles north to Lake Winnipesaukee. Be prepared to pay a large legal fee. "You know," said the local lawyer doing my title search, "that land originally belonged to the Indians. I had to go looking all over for them. I looked in Aspen, Vail, and Sun Valley. They weren't there, so . . ."

And even after you've cleared the title and paid for the house, it won't be called yours. My house is "the Yateman place." There hasn't been a Yateman in Jaffrey for fifty years. And I don't think a Yateman ever owned my house anyway. "The Yateman place" is just a device to rag newcomers. Though I have been assured that my house will eventually be called "the O'Rourke place."

"Everybody'll call it that," said a neighbor, "just as soon as you die there."

Another thing, no matter how stately the home or how much land or how many outbuildings, the only thing the natives will ever say about it is, "You know that place sold for eight thousand in 1976."

It will take time for you to get used to these country ways, not to mention getting used to the country itself. The climate, for instance—we have two seasons in New England, winter and getting-ready-for-winter. I was used to banging on my apartment building's pipes when I wanted more heat in the middle of the night.

P. J. O'Rourke

I've found this doesn't work with my own wood furnace. Nor are municipal services exactly like the city's. I was putting trash out at the end of my driveway for three months before I noticed . . . well, I noticed three months' worth of trash out at the end of my driveway.

Just running simple errands is a problem for transplanted New Yorkers. We are brusque, fast-moving people. But there's an unwritten law in New England: Anytime you go anywhere to conduct any type of business, first you have to have a little talk.

When you go to the butcher shop, you're not going there to buy meat. It's a social call. Even if you've never seen the butcher before, you say, "How's it going?" and "Come on by sometime" and "Give my regards to your wife if you're married."

He'll say, "Black flies bad up at your place this year?"

You'll say, "Getting any wood in?"

And so on. Anything to do with pot roast is strictly incidental, and the subject cannot be raised politely for at least thirty minutes.

This frightens me. I know people do it to be friendly. I try to talk for hours with everyone I see. But I'm scared that if I call the fire department and yell "Help! My house is on fire!" I'll get someone on the other end of the line saying, "Ah-yep, fellow down at Antrim had his house on fire too. Must have been just about this time, 1981. Black flies bad up at your place this year?"

The local newspapers are a great help in catching the spirit of country life. These publications show that rural New Englanders live in a different world than New Yorkers, possible on a different planet.

I've been collecting items from the papers in my area. This headline was printed large on page one of the *Monadnock Ledger:* "Spaghetti Supper Set for Friday." It's the sort of headline we could do with more of in the *New York Post.* "Motorist Damages Yard in Hit and Run Accident"—that appeared on the front page of the *Peterborough Transcript.* And here, from the *Keene Sentinel,* is my personal favorite: "Maine Legislature Goes Home."

A story about the planning board in Jaffrey read, in part, "The

201

planners did not decide on the subdivision last week. By the time
the public hearings were over . . . it was after 11:00 P.M. The
planners did not think they should be making decisions when they
were tired." It's hard to imagine Congress being that downright.
I'd like to see a story in the *New York Times* saying, "Congressmen
did not decide on the defense budget last night. The members of
Congress did not think they should be making decisions when they
were half-witted, corrupt, and drunk." But the most telling item
I've found in my local papers read simply, "Money was found on
Middle Hancock Road on Sunday, June 5." Eleven words which
paint a picture of almost baffling decency.

Things like that will make you want to get to know your
neighbors. Believe me, they'll already know you. New Englanders
are not nosy. They pride themselves on respecting the privacy of
others. All the same, they manage to know everything about you,
and sometimes they'll let it slip. You'll be on the phone, making
a long-distance call. "Operator," you'll say, "I'm having trouble
getting through to my mother in Florida."

The operator will say, "You really ought to call her more
often, and you haven't written her a real letter since Christmas."

Or you'll be shopping in a local store and the salesclerk, a
total stranger to you, will say, "But that's not the kind of undershirt
you usually wear."

The first of these neighbors you should get to know is the
plumber. Marry him if you can. In some rural places the most
prominent citizen is the doctor or the reverend at the church; not
so in New England. It's the plumber, and for good reason. When
your water pipes freeze and burst at 3:00 A.M., try calling an M.D.
or a priest.

It will be easier to get to know the plumber, and everyone else,
if you understand local values. One local value is early rising. Don't
let on that you sleep until 10:00. It's considered hilarious. Personally, I sleep in my clothes with a coffee mug beside my bed. That
way, when someone rings the doorbell at 5:00 A.M. to see if I'd like
help stacking cordwood, I can run downstairs with cup in hand and

pretend to have been awake for hours. Getting up early means going to bed early, and it worries people if you don't. When I first moved to Jaffrey, I was having a 1:00 A.M. nightcap when I heard a knock on the door. It was a concerned-looking native in a bathrobe. "We saw your lights on," he said. "Is anything wrong?"

The two most important New England values, however, are honesty and thrift. Honesty you've already seen exampled in Middle Hancock Road where someone found money and did what only a born and bred small-town Yankee would do and called the newspapers. This honesty is a great thing but dangerously habit-forming. On visits to New York I have found myself telling people, "Just charge me what you think is fair." And there is no polite way to express what people in New York think is fair.

More important even than honesty is thrift, not to say outright tight-fistedness. Money in the city is like money in Weimar Germany. You go to the Citibank cash machine, get a wheelbarrowful of the stuff, and shovel it out whenever you're told. Then you cross your fingers and hope to die before the Visa Card people process your change of address. But Yankees are serious about spending money. And they give advice at length on the subject.

"Drive over to Portland, Maine," they'll say, "and you can get two cents off paper towels." Or "There's a special on five-gallon cans of margarine at the A&P. Limit, six to a customer." And they're especially forthcoming with advice about what you should have paid for your house. "You know that place sold for eight thousand in 1976."

Besides changes in values, country life means changes in all your activities. Many city pursuits are inappropriate to the new venue. If you go jogging in Jaffrey, people will stop and offer you a ride. And having dinner at 9:00 is considered as bizarre as sunbathing on a roof. Do not, however, adopt local customs wholesale.

Fishing, for example, turns out to be less serene than it looks on calendars. It is a sport invented by insects and you are the bait.

Hunting is as uncomfortable and much more hazardous. Deer

hunting, particularly, attracts Visigothic types from places like Worcester, Massachusetts. I spend all of deer-hunting season indoors trying not to do anything deerlike.

Gardening is better. Everyone in New England will be eager to give you advice about a flower garden—too eager, in fact. By the time I'd spent a month listening to gardening advice, I was so confused the only thing I could remember was that you shouldn't plant bulbs upside down. This is nonsense, and I have a septic tank full of daffodil blooms to prove it.

Vegetable gardening is even more frustrating. The last hard frost in New England comes about July 10 and the first autumn frost comes about two weeks later. Then there are the raccoons. If anything does grow, the raccoons will take it and you'll have to call the Pentagon Rapid Deployment Force to get it back. What I do is just *say* I have a vegetable garden. I dig up some of the lawn, put on a raccoon suit, make tracks in the dirt, and go buy my vegetables at the local garden stand.

I've adopted similar techniques for home renovation. At first I thought it would be relaxing and a fine hobby to fix up my own house. But visits to the hardware store proved too embarrassing. Whatever it is you need, you don't know what it's called. And they'll laugh at you when you ask for "a large metal thing which is heavy at one end but a good deal heavier at the other."

While being careful not to fix up your own house, be especially careful not to fix it up in real Colonial antiques. There's one place where the honesty of rural New Englanders breaks down in a woeful fashion. This is the antique store. New England antique stores are dens of iniquity. If you ever do go into one, keep repeating this to yourself: "It's *not* an authentic milk-paint pre-Revolutionary hanging cupboard. It's a dirty old box out of somebody's garage."

Moving to the country is, in general, a splendid way of finding out how ignorant and unhandy you are. I knew I didn't know much about gardening or fixing things around the house, but I thought even I could burn a pile of brush. It's worth noting that practically everything in rural areas is flammable. So much for the lovely scenery.

Indeed, by the time I'd lived six months in New England, all my good reasons for moving there had disappeared. Pastoral serenity is elusive in a town where every man, woman, and child over five owns a chain saw and starts it promptly at dawn each day. And as for healthy living, the state motto of New Hampshire seems to be "Can I freshen that up for you?"

I was feeling quite glum about all this one day while I was helping another ex-city fellow pull stumps out of his pasture. My friend George, a former resident of San Diego, had rented a backhoe, and he and I had spent all morning cutting, digging, and yanking at tree roots while I wondered why I'd ever left Murray Hill. George and I were down in a trench hacking at one particularly recalcitrant oak carcass when a local farmer pulled up in his truck. The farmer stared out across the pasture, surveyed the dozen holes with uprooted stumps sitting next to each, looked down in the hole where George and I were, and said, "George, you'll never make any money planting those."

Then I realized why I'd moved to the country. Neighbors gather from miles around to see me try to light a wood stove. My sojourns at the town dump with my Volkswagen convertible buried to its hubs in mud are local legend. And the residents of Jaffrey consider it a better show than *Return of the Jedi* to see a New Yorker try to get a porcupine out of the barn with two oven mitts and a broom handle.

You move to the country for the same reason that underlies many great artistic endeavors. It's done for the sake of entertainment. And what better thing is there in life than bringing mirth and merriment to the people all around you?

The King of Sandusky, Ohio

〜〜〜〜〜〜〜〜〜〜〜〜〜〜〜〜〜〜〜〜〜

My grandfather was King of Sandusky, Ohio. His father, King Mike the First, had ruled a small farm ten miles from town. There was a period of great disorder in Sandusky then, due to the City Ordinance of Succession. The throne of Sandusky cannot pass through a female heir. King Jim, who ruled in the year of my grandfather's birth, 1887, had no sons and no brothers, nor had he had any paternal uncles. So the question of inheritance fell among an array of quarreling cousins, one of whom (though, I believe, only by marriage) was my great-grandfather Mike. But Mike was good with a broadsword and had friends at the county courthouse. Eventually he was appointed Chancellor of the Exchequer at one of the local banks and conquered a lumber yard and a livery stable. King Jim was old and growing senile and my great-grandfather had himself declared Royal Protector by taking care of the old king's house and yard and making sure he always had a carriage if he wanted to go for a ride in the country. When King Jim died in 1901 my great-grandfather knew where all the legal papers were, and, with the help of my young grandfather, the future Crown Prince Barney, he fought a pitched battle with the other claimants and cousins in an office downtown. He was greatly outnumbered by his rivals, but they were leaderless and quarreled among themselves, and while they were consulting a lawyer they had hired, King Mike set upon them with archers and most of them were slain. A few retired on pensions, however, and one moved to California.

King Mike died in 1920, and his oldest son, my great-uncle Will, became King of the Farm, but it was my grandfather who was placed upon the throne of Sandusky. This was not in strict adherence to the Succession Ordinance, but few men ever defied my grandfather and lived or did not have a business failure.

Under the reign of my grandfather, Sandusky grew in power and prosperity. A grain elevator was built and a factory and then another. My grandfather was always at war. He conquered Norwalk, Fremont, Tiffin, and Oak Openings State Park, where there was a battle that lasted nearly two days in the dark and tangled woods of the bird sanctuary. In 1942 he defeated Port Clinton, using archers—as his father had—and massed infantry armed with pikes and swords at the bridge on Route 4. The mounted knights he fought, whose number made up nearly all the nobility and royal family of Port Clinton, were shot down with arrows or forced over the guardrail and drowned in their heavy armor before anyone could get to them with a powerboat. It's a lesson I've never forgotten. Cavalry is important for mobility's sake and for swift forays, but the true strength of an army lies in its well-trained foot soldiers. Also horses have to be fed and groomed every day and usually boarded at a stable on the outskirts of town.

King Barney commissioned a navy for Sandusky, with three-masted galleons. And he fought sea battles at Put-In Bay, at North Bass Island, and even at the mouth of the Maumee River, in Toledo harbor. Thus my grandfather wrested much of the freighter traffic in western Lake Erie from the Businessmen Princes of Toledo and Detroit, Michigan. He also fended off attacks from the barbarians who came down out of Canada in their war ferries. They wore no armor, only hats, and fought with axes, but they were fearsome warriors nonetheless and were driven from our shores only after they had sacked many fishing camps and a boat dock. There was an uprising, too, among the peasants who were in a labor union at the Willis Overland plant, and my grandfather put down that rebellion with great force. And he quarreled with the deacon of the largest Presbyterian church in town, a man who commanded powerful forces and wanted to enforce the Eighteenth Amendment, which commanded Prohibition and caused a great schism in Ohio. My grandfather, at last, seized all the deacon's property and foreclosed on some empty lots and small businesses that he owned, distributing them with his customary largess to the earls and counts who owned restaurants and bars and had fought loyally by the king's side. He took for himself a Buick dealership. And built a palace for the royal household on Elm Street. By the time I was born, in 1957, King Barney ruled nearly all of north-central Ohio from Lorraine to Bucyrus and as far west as Perrysburg. What he hadn't conquered by sword and fire had been annexed by the city government, and dukes and barons from surrounding towns swore fealty to my grandfather, even, in some cases, sending their own children as hostages on vacation visits to the royal court. Where, of course, they were treated with the greatest courtesy.

King Barney, though fierce in war, was at heart a kindly man, loved by his subjects. Very few were the times when he threw anyone into the dungeon at the Buick dealership, and only then when they had commited some heinous crime. And he hated to order an execution. Even when Lenord of Fostoria married my second cousin, Duchess Connie, and treated her cruelly, and was cast into the dungeon and broke $300 worth of distributor caps and taillight lenses which were stored there, Grandfather did not have him killed but just talked him into joining the Marine Corps.

211

Republican Party Reptile

My grandfather, King Barney, had five children. Crown Prince Bob was the oldest; then my father, who bore the title Prince of New Car Sales and was also the Captain of the Royal Guard; then Princess Annie; then Prince Larry, who ran the used-car lot; and my youngest uncle, Prince Fred. My father married Princess Doris, whose father had been the Emperor of Michigan City, Indiana, but who had been deposed in the stock-market crash of 1929. Her family had fled Indiana, and her brother Sam took refuge in a monastery owned by the New York Central Railroad, where he became Chief Abbot and a freight-train engineer. Her sister Dorothy married a real-estate salesman from Chicago who was very successful because he was the duke of a suburb.

I led an idyllic childhood, partly at the court of my grandfather the king and partly at his summer cottage. I was trained in the arts of warfare and at falconry and baseball and playing the trumpet. My father was a great favorite with the people. It was assumed that someday he would be king, since Uncle Bob had no male heirs. Oddly, I must have been nearly ten before I realized that I myself was therefore in line for the crown. And it was not long after I had made that realization that my father was tragically struck down. There had been trouble at the car dealership. A White Castle restaurant across the street had rebelled, and my father and my Uncle Larry, who was his chief lieutenant, gathered their troops and some of the mechanics from the garage and laid siege to the Amazon waitresses. It was only a glancing blow of a halberd that struck my father's helmet, and Prince Larry told me that in the victorious glow of the burning lunchroom my father complained of nothing but a slight headache. But that night he suffered a cerebral hemorrhage and went into the hospital and died. A hundred lancers on horseback and many people in a long line of cars accompanied him to his grave in Woodlawn Cemetery, where our family owned a plot.

Less than a year later my mother married again, to Count Ralph, a minor nobleman from a shopping center on the south side of town. And thus began the intrigue that was to mark the next dozen years of my life.

P. J. O'Rourke

At first I didn't care much one way or the other about my new stepfather. He seemed nice enough, in a way, but he drank too much beer and his armor was the cheap foreign kind. And he did not have a charger of his own. Anytime there was an argument with a neighbor over feudal obligations like keeping their lawns nice, he would have to rent a horse in order to settle the quarrel with a jousting match. But I didn't really mind him. Anyway, I was much too busy with the Grade School Wars. They caused great destruction and suffering, especially to substitute teachers. My grandfather should have put a stop to these fights, but he was growing old and he never recovered from the death of my father, who was his favorite. He began to grow feeble after that and wound up in a royal nursing home. And my Uncle Bob, the crown prince, cared about nothing but business and golf.

There were three grade schools in the local school district, and we were at war with each other constantly. And the four public high schools in Wood County were fighting each other, also. Not to mention the two parochial high schools, each of which had elected its own pope. And this caused rioting among the Polish and Italian people who worked in the factories. At school we fought with wooden pikes and swords. Most of our parents wouldn't let us have real swords until we were sixteen. Although some kids who had paper routes saved up and bought them anyway. We had real arrows, though. And I was grazed on the arm once and had to have stitches.

The school wars were exciting. They were fought from classroom to classroom. I was one of the leaders, of course, because I was of royal blood. But I was in the sixth grade, so I was only a lieutenant. Still, I led my men in many sword fights, especially on the staircases. We would fight up and down the staircases. They were the best places for sword fights. Our school, McKinley School, was a big building, like a fortress, and we fought from barricades across the corridors, and even the principal couldn't get us to behave. Once we were besieged by the kids from Nathan Hale Grade School, and they drove us to the second floor and conquered our gym. We might have starved if the girls hadn't had to go home when the streetlights came on. And they were able to get back into the school auditorium that night because there was a PTA meeting and they came with their parents. We hoisted picnic baskets full of provisions up from the auditorium floor to the balcony, and so we survived until morning. We had new sword fights on all the staircases that next day and drove the Nathan Hale kids back to their own neighborhood. We captured one of their sixth-graders, who used to be in my class but his parents moved. He was a spy, and we proved it with a trial by fire, and he died in the hospital. After that our grade school couldn't fly the green safety pennant on our flagpole under my family's royal banner. The green safety pennant meant no student had been hurt that year and had a picture of Amber the Safety Elephant on it.

I was so busy that I didn't notice that Count Ralph, my stepfather, was conspiring against me until my grandfather died and Uncle Bob was crowned King of Sandusky. This made me crown prince, and I always led my class when we marched to school assemblies or to drop our contributions into the March of Dimes collection. Count Ralph's first plot was to poison my uncle so that I would be king and he could be appointed regent until I was twenty-one. He tried this at a weenie roast but King Bob only vomited and the poison hot dog did not have time to do its work.

But then my stepfather decided upon a different and more treacherous scheme. I believe he realized that I knew about the poisoning attempt, for I had spied on him when I worked after school at his hardware store in the shopping center. And he knew I had come to hate him because he would not buy me an English racer bicycle and because he continually ranted and raved at me for not cleaning up after my brace of coursing hounds. He and my uncle came to a rapprochement. And despite my warnings to the king, Count Ralph was made my protector and Head of the Royal Guards. It became clear to me that the two of them were in league when my cousins Prince Buster and Prince Kevin were waylaid on the street and killed by a hit-and-run driver. This left no other male heir but me, and if I could be gotten out of the way, King Bob's grandson, my second cousin Prince Dickie, could be made crown prince. I knew, also, that Count Ralph was aiding my uncle in urging City Council to change the laws of royal succession. Either way I would never become king. They couldn't kill me outright, not yet. It would look bad in the papers. But they were going to get rid of me somehow. My mother was weak. She feared for my safety, but she also wanted to save her marriage and was afraid of what the neighbors would say if she got divorced. I went to my uncles, Prince Larry and Prince Fred, whose sons had been murdered. I asked them for help raising a troop of armed men. I could muster a hundred boys from McKinley School and at least my own patrol from my Boy Scout troop, but we were poorly armed and had no siege engines or cavalry. But my uncles were scared they'd lose their jobs. Only Princess Annie was any help. She gave me a packet of poison to spread on the fabric of my stepfather's sport coat. But I lost it on the way home.

There was nothing to do but flee, so I sought sanctuary at the home of my mother's brother, the Duke of Evanston, Illinois.

This was not a happy time of my life. I was among strangers whose customs and manner of dress were unfamiliar to me. And it was a cliquish high school. I didn't fit in. Then the duke, my uncle, had a massive coronary. I had hoped that he and his son, my cousin Eddie, would help me raise an army. Perhaps, also, Reverend Stevens at Evanston United Methodist would declare a crusade, and I could return to Sandusky and topple Uncle Bob from the throne. Cousin Ed was a bully and I had never liked him, but he had powerful friends on the football team. But my hopes were dashed, and instead of raising an army, I was caught in a quarrel between my cousin, the new duke, and his mother, who still held the purse strings of the ducal treasury at the local branch bank and would not let Duke Eddie have even his own checking account. And Lady Sue, Eddie's sister, was contemplating a totally unsuitable marriage to a commoner, a bread-truck driver. And, worse, this man was a heretic, a Seventh Day Adventist whose family had been slaughtered in the general massacre of Adventists the year before.

Republican Party Reptile

He had escaped only because he had been out in the garage trying to fix a lawnmower when it happened. But he lived in fear for his life and planned to emigrate to the colonies in Wisconsin, where he hoped religious toleration would be found. And he planned to take Lady Sue with him. No one had time for me, and I never did make many friends in school.

Before my senior year, I decided to return alone to Sandusky. I knew I faced likely death or imprisonment in my bedroom on some slight pretext. Nor did I have any plan. Uncle Sam tried to convince me to become a railroad monk. But I must have a life of action, and if I could not find some way to succeed in Sandusky, then perhaps I would become a brigand and live in the forest and rob picnickers.

Once I was home, however, a streak of good fortune came my way. My high school was in the wealthiest part of town, but our athletic teams were not very good and in the various skirmishes and battles with the other schools in the parking lots after football games we had lost many dead and wounded. We had no archers, our single troop of lancers was decimated, and our infantry was a rabble of kids whose parents were not very well off. Because I was still, in name at least, crown prince, it was easy to get elected to Student Council. And since no one else wanted the job, I became chairman of the Battle and Pillage Committee. I knew there was no way that I could form our high school's dispirited and disorganized army into an effective fighting force, not even against other high schools, let alone against my uncle, the king, and my stepfather and his Royal Guards—especially since my stepfather had grounded me for a month for getting a speeding ticket. Still, with even a few troops I had some options open. You see, of the six high schools in the Sandusky area there was one, Scott High, which was nearly all colored. We were at peace with them, just then. And, in fact, since they were in an isolated part of town, they were at war with no one but some eastside rednecks who were high school dropouts anyway. But what I did was bully our Student Council President—a little bespeckled fellow and a great coward—into making belligerent noises toward Scott High on the pretext of a Negro family or two moving into our school district. We could not beat them in a set-piece battle. I knew that. But their school was far enough away from ours that it would not come to outright war for a while, I felt sure. Then, one night, I took a dozen of my best and most trusted swordsmen and we dressed ourselves as colored people, wearing gauntlets and keeping our visors down so that no one could see the true color of our skin. Then I led a small raid on some houses in a nice neighborhood near our school. We burned the places to the ground and killed the families, being sure to perform the worst mutilations on the bodies. It got a lot of coverage on television, and the first result was a much larger military budget for my army. We took, in fact, all the money from the Prom decorations fund—everything that had been made from car washes and bake sales for a whole year. I purchased arms and horses and even a siege engine or two, which did much to raise morale.

The kids at Scott High denied they'd done the killings, of course, and, of course, we called them liars and threatened war. But threats were as far as I let it go just then. Instead of attacking Scott High, my little band of raiders and I made another attack pretending to be colored. This time we attacked houses near Libby High School. My school and Libby had been at war for years, and I thought, rightly, that a "colored" outrage would give us cause to unite with them against the Negros. I won't go on with all the details, but in such a way I eventually brought all five of the white high schools, even the Catholic ones, into a unified force. We made terrible war on the Negros and they, vastly outnumbered, were beaten in battle after battle and driven back into the center of the slum where they lived.

That spring the four other military commanders and I sat in parlay to plan a final attack, a complex action along converging lines, which is the hardest type of battle plan to make. The strategy, drafted by myself, was, if I may say so, excellent. It would take too much time to detail it here, but, briefly, the plan was to use our cavaliers not as the primary fighting force (such as was then the custom among high schools) but for the purpose of continual short feints to turn the Negro flanks between poised companies of our five-school infantry, which I had drilled. And while our archers held the colored center pinned down, we would cut their troops to ribbons from each end. By means of this battle we intended to wipe out all the remaining colored people in Sandusky, for we planned to slaughter the prisoners and children.

I held precedence at this council, by virtue of my inheritance and tactical ability, but I knew that with the end of the colored war we would all fall back to quarreling with each other. And I also knew that some of the other high school commanders had no love for me. At least two, in fact, wanted to command a united army of high school students and use it to take control of the city just as I planned to. Therefore I made a diplomatic move unbeknownst to my comrades in arms. I arranged a secret meeting with the leader of the colored forces. I told him of our intention to massacre his people, and he was very upset about it. But I offered to make an arrangement with him. If he would ensure that his troops killed each of my four co-commanders, then I would allow him to surrender on liberal terms with no massacre or rape or looting by the white armies. He agreed, and I showed to him the exact position that each commander would be occupying during the battle. He swore that he would do his best to see that each was killed.

It was a terrific fight. Every Negro person in Sandusky had armed himself as best he could with knives and shovels and rocks and bottles, and the police had cordoned off that whole part of town so that we could fight without tying up traffic. Of course, the colored troops were no match for our mounted knights, and our archers and crossbowmen cut them down in waves. But they fought well, giving no quarter and asking none. And, while they fought, the captain of their high school's guard fulfilled his promise to me and sent his best knights in at just the place I had told him so that by midafternoon three of my rivals were dead and the other so badly wounded that he had to go home. I alone was left in charge of the field, and when the Negros at last began to wave white bedsheets attached to broom handles and garden rakes, I called a halt to the killing. I gave the colored people a place to live, between the freightyard and the river, on the edge of downtown as far south as the Delco battery plant, and they remain loyal subjects to this day.

Now I was in uncontested command of a battle-seasoned army of three thousand men, and I could have turned them at any time against my stepfather's Royal Guards and won the issue, I had no doubt. But the time was not yet ripe. For one thing it would have been against the law and I might have been sent to reform school if the police caught me doing it. And for another thing, my uncle, though not so popular as his father had been, still had public opinion on his side. The thing to do instead, I thought, was to force King Bob to make *me* head of the Royal Guard, as was my birthright. But that was impossible so long as my protector and stepfather, Count Ralph, lived. Nor did I trust my younger uncles, either of whom might be made protector in his stead. So I had Prince Fred and Prince Larry murdered and would have done the same for Count Ralph. But my stepfather was too well protected for that, and there would have been no doubt in anyone's mind as to who had ordered it done. So I decided to pick a quarrel with him and kill him in a public duel.

It happened at the dinner table. Mom had just brought in the roast when Count Ralph, unhinged by my taunts while we'd been eating salad, drew his rapier and, made clumsy by his anger, thrust into a bowl of potato salad. I leapt on my chair and, grabbing the pull-down light fixture in my left hand, slashed at him with the heavy saber I had carried to the table for just this purpose. I missed and cut one of the dining-room drapes in half. Ralph parried my backstroke and cut me beneath the arm. I kicked a gravy boat at his chest and, as he flinched, caught him with a glancing blow that cut off his ear and killed my sister Jill. He had his dagger out by now, but dagger and rapier were no match for my heavier weapon, and I backed him into the family room, slashing furiously at his bleeding head. He did me some damage, I must say. I was wounded again in the thigh and lost a finger of my left hand to his knife.

Republican Party Reptile

But I laid open his chest right through the sport shirt so that a strip of flesh fell open like a flap. Ralph ran out the back door onto the patio. I could have skewered him then, from behind, but I wanted a death that was face to face. He poked through the screen as I came out after him, and I stumbled off the steps. He would have had me if he'd been quicker, but he was too fat from beer and too soft from sitting watching TV every night. I regained my footing and we went at it for a moment more until I had him backing away into the yard. It was then that he tripped on the lawn chair and fell backward into it like he was sitting down. His head went back, and I gave a mighty slash and severed it from his body.

King Bob had no choice after that but to make me Captain of the Royal Guards. I accused most all of them of corruption, cheating on their income tax, or violating parking regulations, and had them executed. I replaced them with my own soldiers. Now I'm waiting for my uncle to die. I believe Princess Annie is going to poison him. And then I'll be king and move out and get a place of my own and buy a four-wheel-drive Jeep.